John Russell Bartlett

The Soldiers' National Cemetery at Gettysburg

John Russell Bartlett

The Soldiers' National Cemetery at Gettysburg

ISBN/EAN: 9783337307479

Printed in Europe, USA, Canada, Australia, Japan

Cover: Foto ©ninafisch / pixelio.de

More available books at **www.hansebooks.com**

THE
SOLDIERS' NATIONAL CEMETERY

AT

GETTYSBURG.

WITH THE PROCEEDINGS AT ITS CONSECRATION; AT THE LAYING OF THE CORNER-STONE
OF THE MONUMENT, AND AT ITS DEDICATION.

BY

JOHN RUSSELL BARTLETT,

Secretary of the Board of Commissioners.

PROVIDENCE:
Printed by the Providence Press Company, for the Board of Commissioners of the
National Cemetery at Gettysburg.
1874.

CONTENTS.

	PAGE
Origin and History of the Soldiers' National Cemetery at Gettysburg,	1
Letter of Hon. DAVID WILLS to GOVERNOR CURTIN suggesting the purchase of ground for a Cemetery on the Battle Field at Gettysburg,	1
GOVERNOR CURTIN'S Letter in reply,	4
Letter from the Hon. EDWARD EVERETT accepting the invitation to deliver the Oration at the Consecration of the Cemetery,	5
Charter of the Soldiers' National Cemetery from the State of Pennsylvania,	6
Commissioners of the States and the Board of Managers,	10
List of Contributions from the several States,	11
Interments in the Cemetery,	12
List of Regiments in the different Corps of the Army of the Potomac in the Battle of Gettysburg,	13
Description of the Monument to MAJOR-GENERAL JOHN F. REYNOLDS,	17
Transfer of the Soldiers' National Cemetery to the United States,	17
Description of the Gettysburg Monument,	19
Exercises at the Consecration of the National Cemetery,	21
Letter from MAJOR-GENERAL MEADE,	24
Letter from MAJOR-GENERAL WINFIELD SCOTT,	24
Letter from ADMIRAL CHARLES STEWART,	25
Letter from the Hon. S. P. CHASE,	25
Remarks by the Hon. WILLIAM H. SEWARD, Secretary of State,	25
Address by the Hon. EDWARD EVERETT at the Consecration,	27
Hymn composed by B. B. FRENCH, Esq., sung at the Consecration,	58
Dedicatory Address by President Lincoln, at the Consecration,	59
Dirge by JAMES G. PERCIVAL, sung at the Consecration,	60

CONTENTS.

	PAGE
Exercises at the Laying of the Corner-stone of the Monument in the Cemetery,	61
Letter from ANDREW JOHNSON, President of the United States,	64
The Gettysburg Monumental Ode,	65
Oration of MAJOR-GENERAL O. O. HOWARD,	66
Poem by CHARLES G. HALPINE (MILES O'REILLY),	75
Hymn to the Memory of our Fallen Heroes at the Battle of Gettysburg,	80
Remarks of GOVERNOR CURTIN, of Pennsylvania,	81
Exercises at the Dedication of the Soldiers' Monument,	83
Address by MAJOR-GENERAL MEADE at the Dedication of the Soldiers' Monument,	85
Oration of GOVERNOR O. P. MORTON at the Dedication of the Soldiers' Monument,	88
Dedication Ode by BAYARD TAYLOR,	103

PLATES.

	PAGE
VIEW OF THE SOLDIERS' MONUMENT AT GETTYSBURG, (to face title page).	
PORTRAIT OF MAJOR-GENERAL JOHN F. REYNOLDS,	17
PORTRAIT OF MAJOR-GENERAL GEORGE G. MEADE,	82
PLAN OF THE SOLDIERS' NATIONAL CEMETERY AT GETTYSBURG,	12
PLAN OF THE BATTLE FIELD OF GETTYSBURG,	56

ORIGIN AND HISTORY

OF THE

Soldiers' National Cemetery at Gettysburg.

THE memorable battle of Gettysburg took place on the first, second and third days of July, 1863, and on the twenty-first of the same month, David Wills, Esq., a citizen of Gettysburg, addressed the following letter to His Excellency A. G. Curtin, Governor of the State of Pennsylvania:—

GETTYSBURG, *July 24th*, 1863.

To His EXCELLENCY A. G. CURTIN, *Governor*.

DEAR SIR,—Mr. Seymour is here on behalf of his brother, the Governor of New York, to look after the wounded, etc., on the battle field, and I have suggested to him, and also the Rev. Mr. Cross, of Baltimore, and others, the propriety and actual necessity of the purchase of a common burial ground for the dead, now only partially buried over miles of country around Gettysburg.

There is one spot very desirable for this purpose. It is the elevated piece of ground on the Baltimore turnpike, opposite the Cemetery. It is the place where our army had about forty pieces of artillery in action all Thursday and Friday, and for their protection had thrown up a large number of earthworks for the artillerists. It is the point on which the desperate attack was made by the Lousiana Brigades on Thursday evening, when they succeeded in reaching the guns, taking possession of them, and were finally driven back by the Infantry, assisted with the artillery men, with their handspikes and rammers. It was the key to the whole line of our defences, the apex of the triangular line of battle. It is the spot above all others for the *honorable burial* of the dead who have fallen on these fields. There are two lots of ground, together making eight acres, about three and a half acres belonging to Mr. Raffensperger, and four and a half to Mr. Menchy, and I called on them for the purpose of ascertaining whether it could be bought. They would not sell it for any other purpose, but offer to sell it for the purpose named for $200 per acre each. This is not much out of the way, and I think it should be secured at once and the project started. I refer the matter to you for your careful consideration and decision.

In examining the Act of 26th February, 1862, passed the Legislature in 1862, pp. 550-1, I think that both sections of that Act are broad enough to cover this matter, and that the Act contemplates such an arrangement as I have suggested.

Our dead are lying on the fields unburied (that is no grave being dug), with small portions of earth dug up alongside of the body and thrown over it. In many instances arms and legs, and sometimes heads, protrude, and my attention has been directed to several places where the hogs were actually rooting out the bodies and devouring them. And this on Pennsylvania soil, and in many cases the bodies of the patriotic soldiers of our State. Humanity calls on us to take measures to remedy this; and I think that it was in the contemplation of the Legislature of 1862 to remedy such matters, by making provisions for the honorable burial of the dead of our State who may fall on the field.

My idea is for Pennsylvania to purchase the ground at once, so as to furnish a place for the friends of those who are here seeking places for the permanent burial of their fallen ones, to inter them at once, and also be a place for the burial of the hundreds who are dying here in the hospitals. The other States would certainly, through their Legislatures, in co-operation with our own Legislature, contribute towards defraying the expenses of appropriately arranging and decorating the grounds. The graves that are marked on the field would, of course, be properly marked when removed to the Cemetery, and the bodies should be arranged, as far as practicable, in order of Companies, Regiments, Divisions and Corps.

Dr. Winslow, of the United States Sanitary Commission, tells me that the United States Government furnish coffins, and did heretofore furnish a large amount of walnut or locust head-boards, on which the name, etc., was burnt into the wood. If the United States Government would furnish these, I think the bodies could be disinterred and buried in this place for about $3.50 or $4 each.

I hope you will feel justified in authorizing the immediate purchase of this ground, and the removal of the Pennsylvania dead in the field to it. I think that an arrangement can be made with the other States at once for the removal of all the dead, known and unknown. We have a man here who superintended the burial of our dead for General Patrick, and knows where they are, and where the Rebel graves are, so that there would be no mistake in taking up the bodies.

I know the soldiers in the field would feel most grateful for such a proper mark of respect, on the part of our Chief Executive, for his fallen comrades, and the multitude of friends of the fallen dead, at home, would rejoice to know that the bodies of their brave kindred have been properly cared for by our Governor.

You will please favor me with an early answer. If the matter is delayed I am afraid the owners of the land might be operated on by speculators.

With great respect, I remain yours truly,

DAVID WILLS.

Governor Curtin, a few days after the battle, visited Gettysburg, traversed the battle field, and visited the several hospitals in and around that town, for the purpose of perfecting arrangements for alleviating the sufferings and ministering to the wants of the wounded and dying. He readily approved of the plan submitted by Mr. Wills, appointed him agent of the State, and authorized him to open a correspondence at once with the Governors of other States, whose soldiers had been killed in the battle, and whose bodies were buried on the battle field.

Mr. Wills lost no time in entering upon the duties for which he had been appointed. He communicated with the Governors of the loyal States, and took immediate steps for procuring the land necessary for the contemplated Cemetery, the particulars of which were made known to him in the following letter:—

GETTYSBURG, *August 17th*, 1863.

To His EXCELLENCY A. G. CURTIN, *Governor of Pennsylvania.*

SIR,—By virtue of the authority reposed in me by your Excellency, I have invited the co-operation of the several loyal States having soldier-dead on the battle field around this place, in the noble project of removing their remains from their present exposed and imperfectly buried condition, on the fields for miles around, to a cemetery.

The Chief Executives of fifteen out of the seventeen States have already responded, in most instances, pledging their States to unite in the movement; in a few instances, highly approving of the project, and stipulating to urge upon the Legislatures to make appropriations to defray their proportionate share of expense.

I have also, at your request, selected and purchased the grounds for this Cemetery, the land to be paid for by, and the title to be made to, the State of Pennsylvania, and to be held in perpetuity, devoted to the object for which it was purchased.

The grounds embrace about seventeen acres on Cemetery Hill, fronting on the Baltimore turnpike, and extending to the Taneytown road. It is the ground which formed the apex of our triangular line of battle, and the key to our line of defences. It embraces the highest point on Cemetery Hill, and overlooks the whole battle field. It is the spot which should be specially consecrated to this sacred purpose. It was here that such immense quantities of our artillery were massed, and during Thursday and Friday of the battle, from this most important point on the field, dealt out death and destruction to the Rebel army in every direction of their advance.

I have been in conference, at different times, with agents sent here by the Governors of several of of the States, and we have arranged details for carrying out this sacred work. I herewith enclose you a copy of the proposed arrangement of details, a copy of which I have also sent the Chief Executive of each State having dead here.

I have also, at your suggestion, cordially tendered to each State the privilege, if they desire, of joining in the title to the land.

I think it would be showing only a proper respect for the health of this community not to commence the exhuming of the dead, and removal to the Cemetery, until the month of November; and in the meantime the grounds should be artistically laid out, and consecrated by appropriate ceremonies.

I am, with great respect,
Your Excellency's obedient servant,
DAVID WILLS.

PENNSYLVANIA, EXECUTIVE CHAMBER, HARRISBURG, *August 31st*, 1863.

DEAR SIR,—Yours of the 26th instant was duly received, and ought to have been answered sooner, but you know how I am pressed.

I am much pleased with the details for the Cemetery which you have so thoughtfully suggested and will be glad, so far as is in my power, to hasten their consummation on the part of Pennsylvania.

It is of course probable that our sister States, joining with us in this hallowed undertaking, may desire to make some alterations and modifications of your proposed plan of purchasing and managing these sacred grounds, and it is my wish that you give to their views the most careful and respectful consideration. Pennsylvania will be so highly honored by the possession within her limits of this Soldiers' mausoleum, and so much distinguished among the other States by their contributions in aid of so glorious a monument to patriotism and humanity, that it becomes her duty, as it is her melancholy pleasure, to yield, in every reasonable way, to the wishes and suggestions of the States who join with her in dedicating a portion of her territory to the solemn uses of a National sepulchre.

The proper consecration of the grounds must claim our early attention; and, as soon as we can do so, our fellow-purchasers should be invited to join with us in the performance of suitable ceremonies on the occasions.

I am, very respectfully,
Your obedient servant,
A. G. CURTIN.

DAVID WILLS, ESQ.

It will thus be seen that before six weeks had elapsed from the days of the great battle, the land for a cemetery in the most desirable place had been purchased; and fifteen out of the eighteen loyal States which had been invited to co-operate in the movement so promptly set on foot by the State of Pennsylvania, through Governor Curtin and Mr. Wills, responded favorably to the call. These States, through their several Chief Executives, agreed to unite in the movement, and to urge their Legislatures to make appropriations to defray their proportionate share of the expense of carrying out the contemplated work.

Meanwhile, that no time should be lost, Mr. Wills made arrangements with Mr. William Saunders, an eminent landscape gardener, to lay out the grounds in State lots, apportioned in size to the number of marked graves each State had on the battle field. This number was obtained by having a thorough search made for all the graves, and a complete list taken of the several names marked on them. Great care was taken to identify the bodies of the dead. In most instances the names of the occupants of graves were written upon small rough boards with a lead pencil. In others they were identified by letters, papers, receipts, certificates, diaries, memorandum books, photographs, marks on the clothing, belts or cartridge boxes, etc. In this manner, out of 3,564 bodies interred in the Cemetery, the names of 2,585 were ascertained, while 979 remain unknown.

As soon as the grounds were laid out for the Cemetery, the bodies were carefully taken up, placed in separate coffins and re-interred in the places assigned them, so that the soldiers from each State were laid together. A large number of articles were found on the bodies, which aided, in a great measure, to identify them. These were carefully preserved and arranged in a room assigned for the purpose, where the families and friends of the deceased could obtain them upon application. A list of these articles, with the names of the soldiers upon whose bodies they were found, is printed in the Report of the Select Committee relating to the Soldiers' National Cemetery, presented to the Legislature of the State of Pennsylvania, in 1865. A list is also preserved in the register of the dead, at the Cemetery.

CONSECRATION OF THE NATIONAL CEMETERY.

It being deemed advisable to consecrate the Cemetery with appropriate ceremonies, as soon as the bodies were all re-interred, and before the season suitable for such ceremonies had passed, Mr. Wills, as agent for the Governor of Pennsylvania, with the consent of all the Governors, addressed a note to the Honorable Edward Everett, inviting him to join in the ceremonies, and deliver the oration on the occasion, which it was proposed should take place on the 23rd of October following. To this the following reply was received:—

BOSTON, *September 26th*, 1863.

MY DEAR SIR,—I have received your favor of the 23rd instant, inviting me, on behalf of the Governors of the States interested in the preparation of a Cemetery for the soldiers who fell in the great battles of July last, to deliver an address at the consecration. I feel much complimented by this request, and would cheerfully undertake the performance of a duty at once so interesting and honorable. It is, however, wholly out of my power to make the requisite preparation by the 23rd of October. I am under engagements which will occupy all my time from Monday next to the 12th of October, and, indeed, it is doubtful whether, during the whole month of October, I shall have a day at my command.

The occasion is one of great importance, not to be dismissed with a few sentimental or patriotic common-places. It will demand as full a narrative of the events of the three important days as the limits of the hour will admit, and some appropriate discussion of the political character of the great struggle, of which the battle of Gettysburg is one of the most momentous incidents. As it will take me two days to reach Gettysburg, and it will be highly desirable that I should have at least one day to survey the battle field, I cannot safely name an earlier time than the 19th of November. Should such a postponement of the day first proposed be advisable, it will give me great pleasure to accept the invitation.

I remain, dear sir, with much respect,

Very truly yours,

EDWARD EVERETT.

DAVID WILLS, ESQ., *Agent for the National Cemetery.*

In accordance with the wishes of Mr. Everett the dedication took place on the 19th of November, 1863, accompanied by appropriate and imposing ceremonies.

CHARTER OF THE NATIONAL CEMETERY.

The commissioners of the several States having lots in the Cemetery, held their first meeting at Harrisburg, on the 17th of December, 1863. Twelve States were represented, and the remaining five signified their assent in the action of the convention. At this meeting the following plan for holding the land purchased for the Cemetery and its general management was agreed upon.

First. "That the Commonwealth of Pennsylvania shall hold the title to the land which she has purchased at Gettysburg for the Soldiers' National Cemetery, in trust for the States having soldiers buried there, in perpetuity, for the purpose to which it is now applied."

Second. "That the Legislature of Pennsylvania be requested to create a corporation, to be managed by trustees, one to be appointed by each of the Governors of the States represented at the meeting, or which have consented to join in the purchase of the land, and in otherwise carrying out the plans contemplated for the Cemetery; which trustees shall, at their first meeting, be divided into three classes.

The term of office of the first class to be one year; the second, two years; and the third, three years. The vacancies thus occurring to be filled by the several Governors; and the persons thus appointed to fill such vacancies, to hold their office for the term of three years. The corporation to have exclusive control of the Soldiers' National Cemetery."

At this meeting estimates were submitted of the cost of the Cemetery and proposed monument, and the several States appointing trustees, were to be asked to appropriate a sum of money, to be determined by a division of the estimated expenses, according to their representation in Congress, to be expended in defraying the cost of removing and re-interring the dead, and finishing the Cemetery, under the directions of the corporation. A committee was appointed at this meeting to procure designs for a monument to be erected in the Cemetery.

In compliance with the wishes of the Commissioners as above stated, the Commonwealth of Pennsylvania, at the January Session, 1864, passed the following:—

AN ACT TO INCORPORATE THE SOLDIERS' NATIONAL CEMETERY.

WHEREAS, The Commonwealth of Pennsylvania has purchased seventeen acres of land on Cemetery Hill, on the Gettysburg battle field, in the county of Adams, for a Cemetery for the burial of the remains of the soldiers who fell in the battle of Gettysburg, and the skirmishes incident thereto, in defence of the Union, or died thereafter from wounds received in that battle and the skirmishes; therefore,

SECTION 1. *Be it enacted by the Senate and House of Representatives of the Commonwealth of Pennsylvania in General Assembly met, and it is hereby enacted by the authority of the same,* That the titles to the said lands purchased, as set forth in the foregoing preamble, are hereby ratified and confirmed, and shall vest and remain in said Commonwealth, in fee simple, in trust for all the States having soldiers buried in said grounds; and the said grounds shall be devoted in perpetuity to the purpose for which they were purchased, namely: for the burial and place of final rest of the remains of the soldiers who fell in defence of the Union, in the battle of Gettysburg; and, also, the remains of the soldiers who fell at other points north of the Potomac river, in the several encounters with the enemy during the invasion of Lee, in the summer of one thousand eight hundred and sixty-three, or died thereafter in consequence of wounds received in said battle and during said invasion.

SECTION 2. That B. W. Norris, of the State of Maine, —— ——, of the State of New Hampshire; Paul Dillingham, of the State of Vermont; Henry Edwards, of the State of Massachusetts; John R. Bartlett, of the State of Rhode Island; Alfred Coit, of the State of Connecticut; Edward Cooper, of the State of New York; —— ——, of the State of New Jersey; David Wills, of the State of Pennsylvania; Benjamin Deford, of the State of Maryland; John R. Latimer, of the State of Delaware; —— ——, of the State of West Virginia; Gordon Lofland, of the State of Ohio;

John G. Stephenson, of the State of Indiana; Clark E. Carr, of the State of Illinois; W. Y. Selleck, of the State of Wisconsin; Thomas White Ferry, of the State of Michigan; —— ——, of the State Minnesota, being one Commissioner from each State, having soldiers buried in said Cemetery, be and they and their successors are hereby created a body politic in law, under the name, style and title of the SOLDIERS' NATIONAL CEMETERY, and by that name, style and title shall have perpetual succession, and be able and capable in law to have and use a common seal, to sue and be sued, plead and be impleaded, in all courts of law and equity, and to do all such other things as are incident to a corporation.

SECTION 3. The care and management of the grounds referred to in the preamble and first section of this act, are hereby entrusted solely to the commissioners named in the second section of the same, and those hereafter appointed to represent the States therein named, and their successors in office; the said commissioners shall constitute a board of managers, whose duty it shall be, out of funds that may be in the hands of the treasurer of the corporation, by State appropriations, or otherwise, to remove the remains of all the soldiers referred to in the first section of this act, that have not already been removed to the Cemetery, and have them properly interred therein; and, also, to lay out, fence and ornament, to divide and arrange into suitable plots and burial lots, establish carriage ways, avenues and foot-ways, erect buildings, and a monument, or monuments, and suitable marks to designate the graves, and generally to do all other things in their judgment necessary and proper to be done to adapt the ground and premises to the uses for which it has been purchased and set apart.

SECTION 4. The business of the corporation shall be conducted by the commissioners aforesaid, and their successors in office; the said commissioners shall meet within sixty days after the passage of this act, and organize by electing one of their number president; they shall also appoint a secretary and treasurer, and shall have power to employ such other officers and agents as may be needful; they shall require of the treasurer to enter into bonds, to the corporation, in double the probable amount of money that may be in his hands at any one time during his term of office, with two or more sufficient sureties, conditioned for the faithful discharge of his duties, and the correct accounting for and paying over of the money; which said bond or bonds, shall be approved by the court of common pleas of Adams county, and recorded in the office of the recorder of deeds in and for said county; the term of office of the officers of the board of commissioners aforesaid shall expire on the first day of January, of each and every year, or as soon thereafter as their successors may be duly chosen and qualified to act.

SECTION 5. At the first meeting of the commissioners heretofore named, they shall be divided, by lot, into three classes, and the term of office of the first class shall expire on the first day of January, Anno Domini one thousand eight hundred and sixty-five; the second class, on the first day of January, Anno Domini one thousand eight hundred and sixty-six, and the third class on the first day of January, Anno Domini one thousand eight hundred and sixty-seven; the vacancies thus occurring shall be filled by the Governors of the States which the said commissioners represented; and the persons thus appointed to fill such vacancies, shall hold their office, as commissioners aforesaid, for the term of three years. In case of the neglect, or failure, of the Governor of any State, having burial lots in the Cemetery, to fill such vacancy, the board of commissioners may supply the place by appointing a citizen of the particular State which is not represented in the board by reason of such vacancy; any vacancies not yet filled, or hereafter occurring, in the board of commissioners, by death, resignation, or otherwise, shall be filled, by appointment, for the unexpired term, by the Governor of the State which the person represented, or in case of failure by such Governor to make said appointment, then the place shall be supplied as last above indicated; such other States of the Union, not having burial lots in said Cemetery, but that may at any time hereafter desire to be represented in this corporation, shall have the privilege of nominating a commissioner to represent them severally in the board of commissioners, and thereafter pay their proportionate share of the expense of maintaining said Cemetery.

SECTION 6. The board of commissioners shall annually, at the end of each fiscal year, make a report of the condition and management of the Cemetery; which report shall contain a detailed statement of the receipts and expenditures of the corporation, and a copy thereof shall be forwarded to the Governor of each State represented in the corporation. The expenses incident to the removal of the dead, the enclosing and ornamenting the Cemetery, and all the work connected therewith, and its future maintenance, shall be apportioned among the States connecting themselves with the corporation, according to their population, as indicated by their representation in the House of Representatives of the United States.

SECTION 7. The board of commissioners shall adopt such by-laws, rules and regulations, as they may deem necessary for their meetings and government, and for the government of their officers, agents and employés, and for the care and protection of the cemetery grounds, and the property of the corporation: *Provided*, Said by-laws, rules and regulations be not inconsistent with the Constitution and laws of the United States, the Constitution and laws of the Commonwealth of Pennsylvania and this act of incorporation.

SECTION 8. The board of commissioners shall have no power to appropriate any of the funds of the corporation as a compensation for their services as commissioners.

SECTION 9. The grounds and property of said Cemetery shall be forever free from the levy of any State, county, or municipal taxes; and the Commonwealth of Pennsylvania hereby releases, and exempts, the corporation created by this act of Assembly, from the payment of any enrollment tax, or any tax, or taxes, whatever, that might be imposed by existing laws; all the laws of this Commonwealth now in force, or which may hereafter be enacted, for the protection of cemeteries, burial grounds, and places of sepulture, shall apply with full force and effect to the SOLDIERS' NATIONAL CEMETERY, hereby incorporated, immediately from and after the passage of this act.

SECTION 10. The corporation of the SOLDIERS' NATIONAL CEMETERY shall have power to receive appropriations from the United States, and from the State Legislatures, and also devises, and bequests, gifts, annuities, and all other kinds of property, real and personal, for the purposes of the burial of the dead, enclosing and ornamenting the grounds, and maintaining the same, and erecting a monument, or monuments, therein.

HENRY C. JOHNSON, *Speaker of the House of Representatives.*
JOHN P. PENNY, *Speaker of the Senate.*

APPROVED—The twenty-fifth day of March, Anno Domini one thousand eight hundred and sixty-four. A. G. CURTIN.

ORIGIN AND HISTORY OF THE

COMMISSIONERS OF THE STATES AND THE BOARD OF MANAGERS.

The following were the Commissioners of the States composing the first Board of Managers:—

B. W. Norris, Esq., - - Maine.	John R. Latimer, Esq. - - Delaware.
Hon. Ira Perley, Chief Justice, New Hampshire.	(No appointment after his death.)
His Excellency Paul Dillingham,	Benjamin Deford, Esq., - Maryland.
Governor of Vermont.	Hon. Chester W. Hubbard, - West Virginia.
Henry Edwards, Esq., - Massachusetts.	(U. S. House of Representatives.)
Hon. John R. Bartlett,	Col. Gordon Lofland, - - Ohio.
Secretary of State of Rhode Island.	John G. Stephenson, Esq., - Indiana.
Alfred Coit, Esq., - - - Connecticut.	Clark E. Carr, Esq., - - Illinois.
Edward Cooper, Esq., - - New York.	Hon. T. White Ferry, (U. S. Senate), Michigan.
Levi Scobey, Esq., - - - New Jersey.	W. Y. Selleck, Esq., - - Wisconsin.
Hon. David Wills, - - Pennsylvania.	Hon. Alex. Ramsay, (U. S. Senate), Minnesota.

The following changes were subsequently made by the retirement of the first Commissioners:—

Robert H. McCurdy, Esq., was appointed from New York in 1865.
Hon. A. G. Hammond, " " Connecticut " 1865.
Hon. William Hebard, " " Vermont " 1865.
Stephen Coburn, Esq., " " Maine " 1866.
James Drake, Esq., " " Indiana " 1865.
Edward M. Dubois, Esq., " " New Jersey " 1867.
William S. Charnley, Esq., " " Connecticut " 1868.
Charles Northend, Esq., " " Connecticut " 1870.

At the first meeting for the organization of the Board of Trustees, held at Gettysburg, April 6th, 1864, the following officers were chosen: *—

David Wills, of Gettysburg, *President.*
John R. Bartlett, of Providence, *Secretary.*
Samuel R. Russell, of Gettysburg, *Treasurer.*

---

* At this meeting the executive committee elected were John R. Latimer, of Delaware; Benjamin Deford, of Maryland; and Levi Scobey, of New Jersey. On the death of Mr. Latimer, Robert H. McCurdy, of New York, was elected in his place; and Mr. Selleck, of Wisconsin, and Mr. Edwards, of Massachusetts, added to the committee. The executive committee so constituted continued, without change, until the completion of the monument and the surrender of the Cemetery to the United States.

SOLDIERS' NATIONAL CEMETERY AT GETTYSBURG.   11

Executive Committee.
Robert H. McCurdy, of New York.
Benjamin Deford, of Maryland.
Wm. Y. Selleck, of Wisconsin.
Levi Scobey, of New Jersey.
Henry Edwards, of Massachusetts.

Auditing Committee.
Henry Edwards, of Massachusetts.
Gordon Lofland, of Ohio.
John R. Bartlett, of Rhode Island.

Proposals having been invited for designs and estimates for a monument, to be erected within the Cemetery, to the memory of the soldiers who fell in the battles of Gettysburg, through advertisements in newspapers published in New York, Philadelphia, Cincinnati and Boston, a number were submitted. The Trustees, after mature deliberation, gave the preference to that submitted by J. G. Batterson, of Hartford, the plan being for a shaft of granite, with figures of white marble on the four buttresses, and a figure of the same material on the summit of the monument.

The Trustees having determined to enclose the Cemetery grounds with a substantial stone wall, with an iron fence in front, an imposing gateway of granite, a lodge for the keeper, and with headstones to each of the graves, it was found that a sum much larger than that originally anticipated would be necessary. The desire of the Trustees for additional appropriations, upon being made known to the several loyal States, was promptly responded to by them, and the amount required placed at the disposal of the Trustees.

CONTRIBUTIONS OF THE SEVERAL STATES.

The following were the total apportionments made by the Board of Trustees to the several States having dead buried in the Cemetery, the respective sums being in the ratio of their representation in the Congress of the United States, were paid as follows, viz. :—

Maine,	$1,205 30	
New Hampshire,	2,523 18	
Vermont,	2,523 18	
Massachusetts,	8,410 60	
Rhode Island,	1,682 12	
Connecticut,	3,364 24	
New York,	26,072 86	
New Jersey,	4,205 30	
Pennsylvania,	20,185 44	
Delaware,	841 06	
Maryland,	$1,205 30	
West Virginia,	2,523 18	
Ohio,	15,980 14	
Indiana,	9,251 66	
Illinois,	11,771 84	
Michigan,	5,046 36	
Wisconsin,	5,046 36	
Minnesota,	1,682 12	
Total amount,	$129,523 24	

THE CEMETERY AND GROUNDS ADJACENT.

The Cemetery grounds embrace seventeen acres of land, on what is known as "Cemetery Hill," on the west side of the Baltimore turnpike, and adjoining the local burial-ground. It is that on which the centre of our line of battle rested on the second and third days of July, and the most prominent and important position on the whole battle-field. These grounds have been tastefully laid out with walks and lawns by Mr. William Saunders, landscape gardener, of Washington, and planted with trees and shrubs. In the middle and broadest portion is the Cemetery proper; a semi-circle, within which the bodies of the fallen soldiers are interred, and in the centre of which stands the monument, separated by a low belt of shrubbery, from the graves. The head-stones to the graves are all alike, and form a continuous line of granite blocks, rising nine inches above the ground, showing a face or width of eight inches on their upper surface. The name, company and regiment of each soldier is sculptured on the head-stones, thus securing a simple and expressive arrangement, combined with great durability. A plan of the grounds will be found in the volume, by a reference to which, the exact position of the several State lots will be seen.

The entrance to the Cemetery grounds is on the Baltimore turnpike, through a large iron gateway, appropriately ornamented, with an iron fence the whole length of the front. The division line between the soldiers' and the local cemetery is simply a low iron fence, the remainder being enclosed by a substantial stone wall, surmounted with a heaving capping.

On the right of the gateway a lodge has been erected for the keeper of the Cemetery.

The interments in the Soldiers' National Cemetery are as follows:—

Maine, - - - - 104 bodies.	West Virginia, - - - 11 bodies.
New Hampshire, - - 49 "	Ohio, - - - - 131 "
Vermont, - - - - 61 "	Indiana, - - - 80 "
Massachusetts, - - 159 "	Illinois, - - - 6
Rhode Island, - - 12 "	Michigan, - - - 171
Connecticut, - - - 22	Wisconsin, - - - 73 "
New York, - - - 867	Minnesota, - - 52 "
New Jersey, - - - 78	United States Regulars, 138
Pennsylvania, - - 534	Three lots with unknown dead.979
Delaware, - - - 15 "	
Maryland, - - - 22 "	Total, - - - 3,564

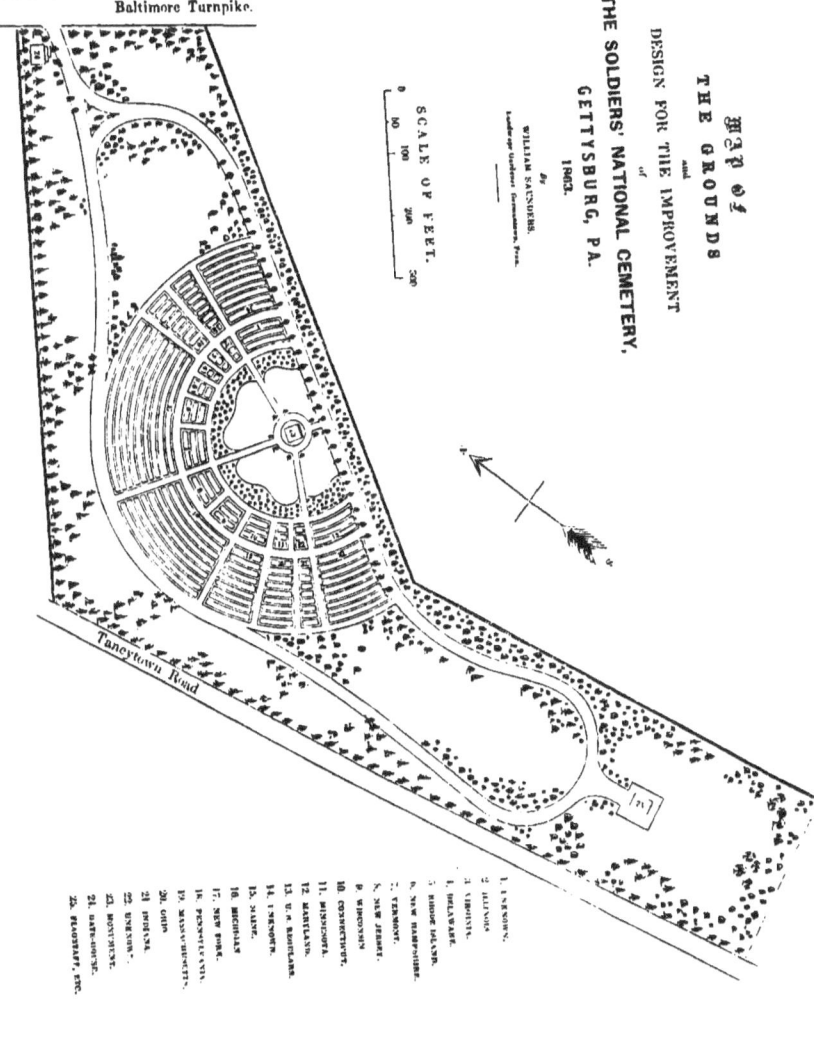

List of Regiments in the different corps of the Army of the Potomac, in the battle of Gettysburg:—

MAINE.

REGIMENT.	CORPS.	REGIMENT.	CORPS.	REGIMENT.	CORPS.
3rd	3rd	6th	6th	17th	3rd.
4th	3rd	7th	6th	19th	2nd.
5th	6th	16th	1st	20th	5th.

NEW HAMPSHIRE.

REGIMENT.	CORPS.	REGIMENT.	CORPS.	REGIMENT.	CORPS.
2nd	3rd	5th	2nd	12th	3rd.

VERMONT.

REGIMENT.	CORPS.	REGIMENT.	CORPS.	REGIMENT.	CORPS.
2nd	6th	6th	6th	14th	1st.
3rd	6th	1st	2nd	15th	1st.
4th	6th	12th	1st	16th	1st.
5th	6th	13th	1st	19th	2nd.

MASSACHUSETTS.

REGIMENT.	CORPS.	REGIMENT.	CORPS.	REGIMENT.	CORPS.
1st	1st	12th	1st	20th	2nd.
2nd	12th	13th	1st	22nd	5th.
7th	6th	15th	2nd	28th	2nd.
9th	5th	16th	3rd	32nd	5th.
10th	6th	18th	5th	33rd	11th.
11th	3rd	19th	2nd	37th	6th.

CONNECTICUT.

REGIMENT.	CORPS.	REGIMENT.	CORPS.	REGIMENT.	CORPS.
5th	12th	17th	11th	20th	12th.
14th	2nd	27th	2nd		

RHODE ISLAND.

2nd Regiment, 6th Corps. 1st Regiment Light Artillery, Batteries A, B and E.

ORIGIN AND HISTORY OF THE

NEW YORK.

REGIMENT.	CORPS.	REGIMENT.	CORPS.	REGIMENT.	CORPS.
9th	1st	64th	2nd	108th	2nd.
14th	1st	65th	6th	111th	2nd.
20th	1st	66th	2nd	119th	11th.
30th	1st	67th	6th	120th	3rd.
33rd	6th	68th	11th	121st	6th.
39th	2nd	69th	2nd	122nd	6th.
40th	3rd	70th	3rd	123rd	12th.
41st	11th	71st	3rd	124th	3rd.
42nd	2nd	72nd	3rd	125th	2nd.
43rd	6th	73rd	3rd	126th	2nd.
44th	5th	74th	3rd	137th	12th.
45th	11th	76th	1st	140th	2nd.
49th	6th	77th	6th	145th	12th.
52nd	2nd	78th	12th	146th	5th.
54th	11th	82nd	2nd	147th	1st.
57th	2nd	86th	3rd	149th	12th.
58th	11th	88th	2nd	150th	12th.
59th	2nd	94th	1st	153rd	11th.
60th	12th	95th	1st	154th	11th.
61st	2nd	97th	1st	157th	11th.
62nd	6th	104th	1st		
63rd	2nd	107th	12th		

PENNSYLVANIA.

REGIMENT.	CORPS.	REGIMENT.	CORPS.	REGIMENT.	CORPS.
P. R. V. C.	5th	75th	11th	114th	3rd.
11th	1st	81st	2nd	115th	3rd.
23rd	6th	82nd	6th	116th	2nd.
26th	3rd	83rd	5th	118th	5th.
27th	11th	84th	3rd	119th	6th.
28th	12th	88th	1st	121st	1st.
29th	12th	90th	1st	134th	11th.
46th	12th	91st	5th	139th	6th.
49th	6th	93rd	6th	140th	2nd.
53rd	2nd	95th	6th	141st	3rd.
57th	3rd	96th	6th	142nd	1st.
61st	6th	98th	6th	143rd	1st.
62nd	5th	99th	3rd	146th	5th.
63rd	3rd	102nd	6th	147th	12th.
68th	3rd	105th	3rd	148th	2nd.
69th	2nd	106th	2nd	149th	1st.
71st	2nd	107th	1st	150th	1st.
72nd	2nd	109th	12th	151st	1st.
73rd	11th	110th	3rd	154th	11th.
74th	11th	111th	12th	155th	5th.

SOLDIERS' NATIONAL CEMETERY AT GETTYSBURG. 15

NEW JERSEY.

REGIMENT.	CORPS.	REGIMENT.	CORPS.	REGIMENT.	CORPS.
1st		7th		12th	
2nd		8th		13th	
3rd		5th		15th	
6th		11th			

DELAWARE.

REGIMENT.	CORPS.	REGIMENT.	CORPS.	REGIMENT.	CORPS.
1st	2nd	2nd	2nd		

MARYLAND.

REGIMENT.	CORPS.	REGIMENT.	CORPS.	REGIMENT.	CORPS.
1st	12th	3rd	12th		

VIRGINIA.

7th Regiment, 2nd Corps.

OHIO.

REGIMENT.	CORPS.	REGIMENT.	CORPS.	REGIMENT.	CORPS.
5th	12th	23rd	11th	75th	11th
7th	12th	29th	12th	82nd	11th
4th	2nd	61st	11th	107	11th
8th	2nd	66th	12th		

ILLINOIS.

82nd Regiment, 11th Corps.

INDIANA.

REGIMENT.	CORPS.	REGIMENT.	CORPS.	REGIMENT.	CORPS.
7th	1st	19th	1st	27th	12th
14th	2nd	20th	1st		

MICHIGAN.

REGIMENT.	CORPS.	REGIMENT.	CORPS.	REGIMENT.	CORPS.
1st	5th	4th	5th	16th	5th.
5th	3rd	7th	12th	24th	1st.

WISCONSIN.

REGIMENT.	CORPS.	REGIMENT.	CORPS.	REGIMENT.	CORPS.
2nd	1st	5th	6th	7th	11th.
3rd	12th	6th	1st	26th	

MINNESOTA.

1st Regiment, 2nd Corps.

UNITED STATES.

REGIMENT.	CORPS.	REGIMENT.	CORPS.	REGIMENT.	CORPS.
2nd sharp sh	3rd	4th Infantry	5th	11th Infantry	5th.
1st "	3rd	6th "	5th	12th "	5th.
2nd Infantry	5th	7th "	5th	14th "	5th.
3rd "	5th	10th "	5th	17th "	5th.

Cavalry Corps.

Maine.—1st Regiment.
Vermont.—1st Regiment.
Massachusetts.—1st Regiment.
Rhode Island.—1st Regiment.
New York.—2nd, 4th, 5th, 6th, 8th, 9th and 10th Regiments.
New Jersey.—1st Regiment.
Pennsylvania.—1st, 2nd, 3rd, 4th, 6th, 8th, 16th, 17th and 18th Regiments.
Virginia.—1st and 3rd Regiments.
Ohio.—6th Regiment.
Indiana.—3rd Regiment.
Illinois.—8th and 12th Regiments.
Michigan.—1st, 5th, 6th and 7th Regiments.
Wisconsin.—1st Regiment.
United States.—1st, 2nd, 5th and 6th Regiments.

Artillery Reserve Corps.

Massachusetts.—5th and 9th Regiments.
New York.—1st Regiment, B and G, 7th Independent, 15th Independent, 30th Independent, 32nd Independent and 1st Independent.
New Jersey.—1st Regiment (A).
Pennsylvania.—1st Regiment (C), 4th Regiment, Independent.
Maryland.—1st and 6th Regiments.
Rhode Island.—1st Regiment Light Artillery (Batteries C and G).
Virginia.—1st Regiment.
Ohio.—1st Regiment (H).
United States.—1st Regiment (H), 3rd Regiment (K), 4th Regiment (C), 4th Regiment (K).

J. J. Reynolds

MONUMENT TO GENERAL JOHN F. REYNOLDS.

Soon after the battle of Gettysburg a desire was expressed to erect a monument to the memory of Major-General John F. Reynolds, who fell early in the contest. To raise the funds necessary for the purpose, a committee of officers, who served in the corps which had been commanded by the deceased general, was appointed. The original subscription was restricted to five dollars from each officer, and fifty cents from each enlisted man, by which means nearly $6,000 was collected.

In 1867, it having been decided to erect a bronze statue to the general, the State of Pennsylvania gave a sufficient number of condemned cannon for the purpose. It was at first contemplated to erect a plain monument of stone on the spot where General Reynolds fell, but when a more imposing memorial was determined upon, the managers of the Soldiers' National Cemetery came forward and appropriated a sum sufficient to construct a foundation and erect a suitable pedestal, upon which to place the statue of General Reynolds within the Cemetery grounds. This amounted to twenty-two hundred dollars. This assistance, with additional subscriptions from officers who had served with the general, enabled the committee to complete the monument.

Upon entering the Cemetery, this beautiful monument meets the eye. It consists of a bronze statue of General Reynolds, of heroic size, standing on a pedestal of dark Quincy granite. The right hand of the general, holding a field glass, hangs at his side, while the left grasps the hilt of his sword. The face is turned towards that part of the field on which the enemy were advancing when he received the fatal shot. The statute was cast at the foundry of Messrs. Robert Wood & Company, Philadelphia, from a design and model by Mr. J. Q. A. Ward, of New York.

TRANSFER OF THE SOLDIERS' NATIONAL CEMETERY TO THE UNITED STATES.

The Cemetery having been completed, and the care of it by Commissioners from so many States being burdensome and expensive, the Board of Managers, on the twenty-second of June, 1871, passed the following preamble and resolutions :—

Whereas, By an Act of the General Assembly of Pennsylvania, passed on the fourteenth of April, 1868, the Commissioners having charge and care of the Soldiers' National Cemetery at Gettysburg, are authorized to transfer all the right, title, interest and care of the said Soldiers' National Cemetery, upon the completion of the same, to the Government of the United States, the Commonwealth of Pennsylvania thereby ceding and relinquishing to the United States all its title to the grounds and property of the said Cemetery vested in it in trust for the States which participated in the establishment of the said National Cemetery, the cession being made upon condition that the United States Government take upon itself the management and care of said Cemetery and make provision for its maintenance: and *whereas* the Cemetery is now completed, and, by a recent Act of Congress, the Secretary of War was empowered and directed to accept and take charge of the Soldiers' National Cemetery at Gettysburg, and the Antietam National Cemetery at Sharpsburg, Maryland, whenever the Commissioners and Trustees having charge of said Cemeteries are ready to transfer their care to the General Government; that when the aforesaid Cemeteries are placed under the control of the Secretary of War, they be taken care of and maintained in accordance with the provisions of the Act of Congress, entitled "An Act to establish and protect National Cemeteries, approved February 22nd, 1867." Now, therefore,

Resolved, That the Commissioners to the said Soldiers' National Cemetery, at Gettysburg, assent and agree to the transfer of the said Cemetery to the Government of the United States according to the provisions of the said Act of the General Assembly of Pennsylvania, and are ready to make the transfer accordingly.

Resolved, That David Wills, Esq., the President of this Board, be, and he hereby is, authorized and empowered, as the Agent of the Board and of the Cemetery, to make transfer of the Cemetery to the proper officer or party authorized to receive the same on the part of the United States, and to do all other acts and things necessary and proper to make and complete the said transfer.

In pursuance of the authority thus conferred on David Wills, he immediately commenced a correspondence with the Secretary of War in reference to the transfer of the care of the Cemetery to the United States. After several conferences the title to the Cemetery was finally made to and accepted by the United States, and on the first of May, 1872, the United States took full and complete possession of the Cemetery, and now has the care and control of it.

Previous to the final adjournment of the Board, on the twenty-second of June, 1871, the members deemed it a duty they owed to the patriotic zeal and energy of David Wills, in the promotion of this work, to put on record an expression of their estimate of his labors, when Judge Perley offered the following resolution, which was unanimously passed:—

Resolved, That the Commissioners to the Soldiers' National Cemetery, being about to deliver over the care of that Institution to the Government of the United States, are unwilling to separate without expressing on the Record our sense of the high value of the services of David Wills, Esq., the President, in conducting the general affairs of the Cemetery. In our judgment it is owing in great measure to his patriotic zeal, to his enterprise, his untiring diligence, his good judgment and taste, that the Commissioners are able to deliver over the Cemetery free from all pecuniary obligation, and in a condition which we are confident will be satisfactory to those for whom we have acted, and to the public.

DESCRIPTION OF THE GETTYSBURG MONUMENT.

The design of the Gettysburg monument is intended to be purely historical, telling its own story, with such simplicity that any discerning mind will readily comprehend its meaning and purpose.

The superstructure is sixty feet high, and consists of a massive pedestal of light grey granite, from Westerly, Rhode Island, twenty-five feet square at the base, and is crowned with a colossal statue of white marble, representing the GENIUS OF LIBERTY. Standing upon a three-quarter globe, she holds with her right hand the victor's wreath of laurel, while with her left she clasps the victorious sword.

Projecting from the angles of the pedestal are four buttresses, supporting an equal number of allegorical statues of white marble, representing respectively, WAR, HISTORY, PEACE and PLENTY.

WAR is personified by a statue of an American soldier, who, resting from the conflict, relates to History the story of the battle which this monument is intended to commemorate.

HISTORY, in listening attitude, records with stylus and tablet, the achievements of the field, and the names of the honored dead.

PEACE is symbolized by a statue of the American mechanic, characterized by appropriate accessories.

PLENTY is represented by a female figure, with a sheaf of wheat and fruits of the earth, typifying peace and abundance as the soldiers' crowning triumph.

These beautiful pieces of statuary, together with the monument, were designed by J. G. Batterson, Esq., of Hartford, Connecticut, and executed in Italy, under the immediate supervision of Randolph Rogers, Esq., the distinguished American sculptor.

The main die of the pedestal is octagonal in form, panelled upon each face. The cornice and plinth above are also octagonal, and are heavily moulded. Upon this plinth rests an octagonal moulded base bearing upon its face, in high relief, the National arms.

The upper die and cap are circular in form, the die being encircled by stars equal in number with the States whose sons gave up their lives as the price of the victory won at Gettysburg.

This monument, as it stands, cost fifty thousand dollars. The purchase of the ground, the removal and re-interring of the dead, the granite headstones, the stone wall and iron fence, the gateway and the porter's lodge, and the laying out and the ornamentation of the grounds, cost about eighty thousand dollars. The " Reynolds Statue" cost ten thousand dollars; thus making the entire cost of the Cemetery, the monument and the Reynolds statue, about one hundred and forty thousand dollars.

EXERCISES

AT THE

Consecration of the National Cemetery at Gettysburg.

NOVEMBER 19th, 1863.

THE CONSECRATION.

THE consecration of the Cemetery was an occasion of deep interest. The public generally were invited to be present and participate in the exercises, and special invitations were sent to the President and Vice-President of the United States and the members of the Cabinet,—to Major-General George G. Meade, commanding the Army of the Potomac, and, through him, to the officers and privates of that army which had fought so valiantly, and gained such a memorable victory on the Gettysburg battle-field,— and to Lieutenant-General Winfield Scott and Admiral Charles Stewart, the distinguished and time-honored representatives of the Army and Navy. Abraham Lincoln, the President of the United States, was present, and participated in the solemnities, delivering a brief Dedicatory Address. The occasion was further made memorable by the presence of large representations from the Army and Navy, of the Secretary of State of the United States, the Ministers of France and Italy, the French Admiral, and other distinguished foreigners, and several members of Congress; also of the Governors of a large number of the States interested, with their staffs, and, in some instances, large delegations, besides a vast concourse of citizens from all the States.

Letters were received, in reply to the invitations addressed to them, from Major-General Meade, Lieutenant-General Scott, Admiral Stewart, and the Secretary of the Treasury, Hon. Salmon P. Chase, regretting their inability to be present, and expressive of their approval of the project.

One of the most sad and impressive features of the solemnities of the nineteenth of November, was the presence, in the procession and on the grounds, of a delegation of about fifty wounded soldiers of the Army of the Potomac, from the York Hospital.

These men had been wounded in the battle of Gettysburg, and were present in a delegation to pay this just tribute to the remains of their fallen comrades. These scarred veterans came and dropped the tear of sorrow on the last resting-place of those companions by whose sides they had so nobly fought, and, lingering over the graves after the crowd had dispersed, slowly went away, strengthened in their faith in a nation's gratitude.

LETTERS OF GEN. MEADE, GEN. SCOTT, ADMIRAL STEWART, AND S. P. CHASE.

HEAD-QUARTERS ARMY OF THE POTOMAC, *November 13th*, 1863.

DAVID WILLS, ESQ., *Agent for the Governor of Pennsylvania, etc.:*

SIR,—I have the honor to acknowledge the invitation which, on behalf of the Governor of Pennsylvania and other States interested, you extend to me and the officers and men of my command, to be present on the nineteenth instant, at the consecration of the burial-place of those who fell on the field of Gettysburg.

It seems almost unnecessary for me to say that none can have a deeper interest in your good work than comrades in arms, bound in close ties of long association and mutual confidence and support with those to whom you are paying this last tribute of respect; nor could the presence of any be more appropriate than that of those who stood side by side in the struggle, shared the peril, and the vacant places in whose ranks bear sad testimony to the loss they have sustained. But this army has duties to perform which will not admit of its being represented on the occasion; and it only remains for me in its name, with deep and grateful feelings, to thank you and those you represent for your tender care of its heroic dead, and for your patriotic zeal, which, in honoring the martyr, gives a fresh incentive to all who do battle for the maintenance of the integrity of the government.

I am, very respectfully, your obedient servant,

GEORGE G. MEADE,

Major-General Commanding.

NEW YORK, *November 19th*, 1863.

DAVID WILLS, ESQ., *Agent, etc.:*

DEAR SIR,—I have had the honor to receive your invitation, on the part of the Governors of the loyal States, to be present at the consecration of the Military Cemetery at Gettysburg, this day.

Besides the determination, on account of infirmities, never again to participate in any public meeting or entertainment, I was too sick at the time to do more than write a short telegram in reply to His Excellency Governor Curtin.

Having long lived with and participated in the hardships and dangers of our soldiers, I can never fail to honor

" the brave, who sink to rest,
By all their country's wishes blest."

None deserve this tribute from their countrymen more than those who have fallen in defence of the Constitution and Union of the thirty-four United States.

I remain yours most respectfully.

WINFIELD SCOTT.

BORDENTOWN, N. J., *November 21st, 1863.*

MY DEAR SIR.—I regret extremely that, in consequence of the invitation you did me the honor to send me remaining for several days among the advertised letters in the Philadelphia post-office, I was not able to accept the same by appearing in person at the interesting consecration of the National Cemetery at Gettysburg, on the nineteenth of this month.

On an occasion so solemn, awakening every patriotic emotion of the human heart, I cannot but deplore that I was not able to be present, to shed a tear over the remains of these gallant men, who gave by their lives to their God in defence of their country.

Accept for yourself, my dear sir, and be pleased to present to the Committee, my thanks for your kind invitation, and believe me, with great respect,

Your obedient servant,

CHARLES STEWART.

To DAVID WILLS, Esq., *Agent, etc.*

TREASURY DEPARTMENT, *November 16th, 1863.*

DEAR SIR,—It disappoints me greatly to find that imperative public duties make it impossible for me to be present at the consecration of the grounds selected as the last resting-place of the soldiers who fell in battle for their country at Gettysburg. It consoles me to think what tears of mingled grief and triumph will fall upon their graves, and what benedictions of the country saved by their heroism will make their memories sacred among men.

Very respectfully yours,

S. P. CHASE.

DAVID WILLS, Esq., *Agent for the Governors of the States.*

REMARKS BY THE HON. WILLIAM H. SEWARD, SECRETARY OF STATE.

In the afternoon of the eighteenth, the President and the distinguished personages accompanying him arrived at Gettysburg by a special train. In the course of the evening, the President and Secretary of State were serenaded, and the following remarks were made by Mr. Seward, in response to the call:—

FELLOW-CITIZENS: I am now sixty years old and upward; I have been in public life practically forty years of that time, and yet this is the first time that ever any people or community so near to the border of Maryland was found willing to listen to my voice; and the reason was that I saw, forty years ago, that slavery was opening before this people a graveyard that was to be filled with brothers falling in mutual political combat. I knew that the cause that was hurrying the Union into this dreadful strife was slavery; and when during all the intervening period I elevated my voice, it was to warn the people to remove that cause while they could by constitutional means, and so avert the catastrophe of civil war which has fallen upon the nation. I am thankful that you are willing to hear me at last. I thank my God that I believe this strife is going to end in the removal of that evil which ought to have been removed by deliberate councils and peaceful means (good). I thank my God for the hope that this is the last fratricidal war which will fall upon the country which is vouchsafed to us by Heaven,—the richest, the broadest, the most beautiful, the most magnificent and capable of a great destiny, that has ever been given to any part of the human race (applause). And I thank Him for the hope that when that cause is removed, simply by the operation of abolishing it, as the origin and agent of the treason that is without justification and without parallel, we shall thenceforth be united, be only one country, having only one hope, one ambition, and one destiny (applause). To-morrow, at least, we shall feel that we are not enemies, but that we are friends and brothers, that this Union is a reality, and we shall mourn together for the evil wrought by this rebellion. We are now near the graves of the misguided, whom we have consigned to their last resting-place, with pity for their errors, and with the same heart full of grief with which we mourn over a brother by whose hand, raised in defence of his government, that misguided brother perished.

When we part to-morrow night, let us remember that we owe it to our country and to mankind that this war shall have for its conclusion the establishing of the principle of democratic government,—the simple principle that whatever party, whatever portion of the community, prevails by constitional suffrage in an election, that party is to be respected and maintained in power until it shall give place, on another trial and another verdict, to a different portion of the people. If you do not do this, you are drifting at once and irresistibly to the very verge of universal, cheerless, and hopeless anarchy. But with that principle this government of ours— the purest, the best, the wisest, and the happiest in the world—must be, and, so far as we are concerned, practically will be, immortal (cheers). Fellow-citizens, good night.

The military present at the exercises on the nineteenth of November, were under the command of Major-General Couch.

The prayer of consecration was made by the Rev. Dr. Stockton.

ADDRESS OF THE HONORABLE EDWARD EVERETT.

Standing beneath this serene sky, overlooking these broad fields now reposing from the labors of the waning year, the mighty Alleghanies dimly towering before us, the graves of our brethren beneath our feet, it is with hesitation that I raise my poor voice to break the eloquent silence of God and Nature. But the duty to which you have called me must be performed:—grant me, I pray you, your indulgence and your sympathy.

It was appointed by law in Athens, that the obsequies of the citizens who fell in battle should be performed at the public expense, and in the most honorable manner. Their bones were carefully gathered up from the funeral pyre, where their bodies were consumed, and brought home to the city. There, for three days before the interment, they lay in state, beneath tents of honor, to receive the votive offerings of friends and relatives,—flowers, weapons, precious ornaments, painted vases (wonders of art, which after two thousand years adorn the museums of modern Europe),—the last tributes of surviving affection. Ten coffins of funereal cypress received the honorable deposit, one for each of the tribes of the city, and an eleventh in memory of the unrecognized, but not therefore unhonored, dead, and of those whose remains could not be recovered. On the fourth day the mournful procession was formed; mothers, wives, sisters, daughters, led the way, and to them it was permitted by the simplicity of ancient manners to utter aloud their lamentations for the beloved and the lost; the male relatives and friends of the deceased followed; citizens and strangers closed the train. Thus marshalled, they moved to the place of interment in that famous Ceramicus, the most beautiful suburb of Athens, which had been adorned by Cimon, the son of Miltiades, with walks and fountains and columns,— whose groves were filled with altars, shrines, and temples,—whose gardens were kept for ever green by the streams from the neighboring hills, and shaded with the trees sacred to Minerva and coeval with the foundation of the city.—whose circuit enclosed

> "the olive grove of Academe,
> Plato's retirement, where the Attic bird
> Trilled his thick-warbled note the summer long."—

whose pathways gleamed with the monuments of the illustrious dead, the work of the most consummate masters that ever gave life to marble. There, beneath the overarching plane-trees, upon a lofty stage erected for the purpose, it was ordained that a funeral oration should be pronounced by some citizen of Athens, in the presence of the assembled multitude.

Such were the tokens of respect required to be paid at Athens to the memory of those who had fallen in the cause of their country. For those alone who fell at Marathon a peculiar honor was reserved. As the battle fought upon that immortal field was distinguished from all others in Grecian history for its influence over the fortunes of Hellas,—as it depended upon the event of that day whether Greece should live, a glory and a light to all coming time, or should expire, like the meteor of a moment; so the honors awarded to its martyr-heroes were such as were bestowed by Athens on no other occasion. They alone of all her sons were entombed upon the spot which they had forever rendered famous. Their names were inscribed upon ten pillars erected upon the monumental tumulus which covered their ashes (where, after six hundred years, they were read by the traveller Pausanias), and although the columns, beneath the hand of time and barbaric violence, have long since disappeared, the venerable mound still marks the spot where they fought and fell.—

> "That battle-field where Persia's victim-horde
> First bowed beneath the brunt of Hellas' sword."

And shall I, fellow-citizens, who, after an interval of twenty-three centuries, a youthful pilgrim from the world unknown to ancient Greece, have wandered over that illustrious plain, ready to put off the shoes from off my feet, as one that stands on holy ground,—who have gazed with respectful emotion on the mound which still protects the dust of those who rolled back the tide of Persian invasion, and rescued the land of popular liberty, of letters, and of arts, from the ruthless foe,—stand unmoved over the graves of our dear brethren, who so lately, on three of those all-important days which decide a nation's history,—days on whose issue it depended whether this august republican Union, founded by some of the wisest statesmen that ever lived, cemented with the blood of some of the purest patriots that ever died, should perish or endure,—rolled back the tide of an invasion, not less unprovoked, not less ruthless, than that which came to plant the dark banner of Asiatic despotism and slavery on the free soil of Greece! Heaven forbid! And could I prove so insensible to every prompting of patriotic duty and affection, not only would you, fellow-citizens, gathered many of you from distant States, who have come to take part in these pious offices of gratitude,—you, respected fathers, brethren, matrons, sisters, who surround me,—cry out for shame, but the forms of brave and patriotic men who fill these honored graves would heave with indignation beneath the sod.

We have assembled, friends, fellow-citizens, at the invitation of the Executive of the great central State of Pennsylvania, seconded by the Governors of seventeen other loyal States of the Union, to pay the last tribute of respect to the brave men, who, in the hard-fought battles of the first, second, and third days of July last, laid down their lives for the country on these hill-sides and the plains before us, and whose remains have been gathered into the Cemetery which we consecrate this day. As my eye ranges over the fields whose sods were so lately moistened by the blood of gallant and loyal men, I see, as never before, how truly it was said of old that it is sweet and becoming to die for one's country. I feel, as never before, how justly, from the dawn of history to the present time, men have paid the homage of their gratitude and admiration to the memory of those who nobly sacrifice their lives that their fellowmen may live in safety and in honor. And if this tribute were ever due, when, to whom, could it be more justly paid than to those whose last resting-place we this day commend to the blessing of Heaven and of men?

For consider, my friends, what would have been the consequences to the country, to yourselves, and to all you hold dear, if those who sleep beneath our feet, and their gallant comrades who survive to serve their country on other fields of danger, had failed in their duty on those memorable days. Consider what, at this moment, would be the condition of the United States, if that noble Army of the Potomac, instead of gallantly and for the second time beating back the tide of invasion from Maryland and Pennsylvania, had been itself driven from these well-contested heights, thrown back in confusion on Baltimore, or trampled down, discomfited, scattered to the four winds. What, in that sad event, would not have been the fate of the Monumental City, of

Harrisburg, of Philadelphia, of Washington, the capitol of the Union, each and every one of which would have lain at the mercy of the enemy, accordingly as it might have pleased him, spurred by passion, flushed with victory, and confident of continued success, to direct his course?

For this we must bear in mind,—it is one of the great lessons of the war, indeed of every war, that it is impossible for a people without military organization, inhabiting the cities, towns and villages of an open country, including of course the natural proportion of non-combatants of either sex and of every age, to withstand the inroad of a veteran army. What defence can be made by the inhabitants of villages mostly built of wood, of cities unprotected by walls, nay, by a population of men, however high-toned and resolute, whose aged parents demand their care, whose wives and children are clustering about them, against the charge of the war-horse whose neck is clothed with thunder,—against flying artillery and batteries of rifled cannon planted on every commanding eminence,—against the onset of trained veterans led by skilful chiefs? No, my friends, army must be met by army, battery by battery, squadron by squadron; and the shock of organized thousands must be encountered by the firm breasts and valiant arms of other thousands, as well organized and as skilfully led. It is no reproach, therefore, to the unarmed population of the country to say, that we owe it to the brave men who sleep in their beds of honor before us, and to their gallant surviving associates, not merely that your fertile fields, my friends of Pennsylvania and Maryland, were redeemed from the presence of the invader, but that your beautiful capitals were not given up to threatened plunder, perhaps laid in ashes, Washington seized by the enemy, and a blow struck at the heart of the nation.

Who that hears me has forgotten the thrill of joy that ran through the country on the Fourth of July,—auspicious day for the glorious tidings, and rendered still more so by the simultaneous fall of Vicksburg,—when the telegraph flashed through the land the assurance from the President of the United States that the Army of the Potomac, under General Meade, had again smitten the invader! Sure I am, that, with the ascriptions of praise that rose to Heaven from twenty millions of freemen, with the acknowledgments that breathed from patriotic lips throughout the length and breadth of America, to the surviving officers and men who had rendered the country this inestimable service, there beat in every loyal bosom a throb of tender and sorrowful gratitude to the martyrs who had fallen on the sternly contested field. Let a nation's fervent thanks make some amends for the toils and sufferings of those who survive. Would that the heartfelt tribute could penetrate these honored graves!

In order that we may comprehend, to their full extent, our obligations to the martyrs and surviving heroes of the Army of the Potomac, let us contemplate for a few moments the train of events, which culminated in the battles of the first days of July. Of this stupendous rebellion, planned, as its originators boast, more than thirty years ago, matured and prepared for during an entire generation, finally commenced because for the first time since the adoption of the Constitution, an election of President had been effected without the votes of the South (which retained, however, the control of the two other branches of the government), the occupation of the national capital, with the seizure of the public archives and of the treaties with foreign powers, was an essential feature. This was in substance, within my personal knowledge, admitted, in the winter of 1860–61, by one of the most influential leaders of the rebellion; and it was fondly thought that this object could be effected by a bold and sudden movement on the fourth of March, 1861. There is abundant proof, also, that a darker project was contemplated, if not by the responsible chiefs of the rebellion, yet by nameless ruffians, willing to play a subsidiary and murderous part in the treasonable drama. It was accordingly maintained by the Rebel emissaries in England, in the circles to which they found access, that the new American Minister ought not, when he arrived, to be received as the envoy of the United States, inasmuch as before that time Washington would be captured, and the capital of the nation and the archives and muniments of the government would be in the possession of the Confederates. In full accordance also with this threat, it was declared by the Rebel Secretary of War, at Montgomery, in the presence of his Chief and of his colleagues, and of five thousand hearers, while the tidings of the assault on Sumter were travelling over the wires on that fatal twelfth of April, 1861, that before the end of May "the flag which then flaunted the breeze," as he expressed it, "would float over the dome of the Capitol at Washington."

At the time this threat was made, the rebellion was confined to the cotton-growing States, and it was well understood by them, that the only hope of drawing any of the other slave-holding States into the conspiracy was in bringing about a conflict of arms, and "firing the heart of the South" by the effusion of blood. This was declared by the Charleston press to be the object for which Sumter was to be assaulted; and the emissaries sent from Richmond, to urge on the unhallowed work, gave the promise, that, with the first drop of blood that should be shed, Virginia would place herself by the side of South Carolina.

In pursuance of this original plan of the leaders of the rebellion, the capture of Washington has been continually had in view, not merely for the sake of its public buildings, as the capital of the Confederacy, but as the necessary preliminary to the absorption of the Border States, and for the moral effect in the eyes of Europe of possessing the metropolis of the Union.

I allude to these facts, not perhaps enough borne in mind, as a sufficient refutation of the pretence on the part of the Rebels, that the war is one of self-defence, waged for the right of self-government. It is in reality a war originally levied by ambitious men in the cotton-growing States, for the purpose of drawing the slave-holding Border States into the vortex of the conspiracy, first by sympathy,—which in the case of Southeastern Virginia, North Carolina, part of Tennessee, and Arkansas, succeeded,—and then by force, and for the purpose of subjugating Maryland, Western Virginia, Kentucky, Eastern Tennessee, and Missouri; and it is a most extraordinary fact, considering the clamors of the Rebel chiefs on the subject of invasion, that not a soldier of the United States has entered the States last named, except to defend their Union-loving inhabitants from the armies and guerillas of the Rebels.

In conformity with these designs on the city of Washington, and notwithstanding the disastrous results of the invasion of 1862, it was determined by the Rebel government last summer to resume the offensive in that direction. Unable to force the passage of the Rappahannock where General Hooker, notwithstanding the reverse at Chancellorsville in May, was strongly posted, the Confederate general resorted to strategy. He had two objects in view. The first was, by a rapid movement northward, and by manœuvring with a portion of his army on the east side of the Blue Ridge, to tempt Hooker from his base of operations, thus leading him to uncover the approaches to Washington, to throw it open to a raid by Stuart's cavalry, and to enable Lee, himself to cross the Potomac in the neighborhood of Poolesville and thus fall upon the capital. This plan of operation was wholly frustrated. The design of the Rebel general was promptly discovered by General Hooker, and, moving with great rapidity from Fredericksburg, he preserved unbroken the inner line, and stationed the various corps of his army at all the points protecting the approach to Washington, from Centreville up to Leesburg. From this vantage-ground the Rebel general in vain attempted to draw him. In the mean time, by the vigorous operations of Pleasanton's cavalry, the cavalry of Stuart, though greatly superior in numbers, was so crippled as to be disabled from performing the part assigned it in the campaign. In this manner General Lee's first object, namely, the defeat of Hooker's army on the south of the Potomac and a direct march on Washington, was baffled.

The second part of the Confederate plan, which is supposed to have been undertaken in opposition to the views of General Lee, was to turn the demonstration northward into a real invasion of Maryland and Pennsylvania, in the hope, that, in this way, General Hooker would be drawn to a distance from the capital, and that some opportunity would occur of taking him at disadvantage, and, after defeating his army, of making a descent upon Baltimore and Washington. This part of General Lee's plan, which was substantially the repetition of that of 1862, was not less signally defeated, with what honor to the arms of the Union the heights on which we are this day assembled will forever attest.

Much time had been uselessly consumed by the Rebel general in his unavailing attempts to out-manœuvre General Hooker. Although General Lee broke up from Fredericksburg on the third of June, it was not till the twenty-fourth that the main body of his army entered Maryland. Instead of crossing the Potomac, as he had intended, east of the Blue Ridge, he was compelled to do it at Shepherdstown and Williamsport, thus materially deranging his entire plan of campaign north of the river. Stuart, who had been sent with his cavalry to the east of the Blue Ridge, to guard the passes of the mountains, to mask the movements of Lee, and to harass the Union general in crossing the river, having been very severely handled by Pleasanton at Beverly Ford, Aldie, and Upperville, instead of being able to retard General Hooker's advance, was driven himself away from his connection with the army of Lee, and cut off for a fortnight from all communication with it,—a circumstance to which General Lee, in his report, alludes more than once, with evident displeasure. Let us now rapidly glance at the incidents of the eventful campaign.

A detachment from Ewell's corps, under Jenkins, had penetrated, on the fifteenth of June, as far as Chambersburg. This movement was intended at first merely as a demonstration, and as a marauding expedition for supplies. It had, however, the salutary effect of alarming the country; and vigorous preparations were made, not only by the General Government, but here in Pennsylvania and in the sister States, to repel the inroad. After two days passed at Chambersburg, Jenkins, anxious for his communications with Ewell, fell back with his plunder to Hagerstown. Here he remained for several days, and then, having swept the recesses of the Cumberland valley, came down upon the eastern flank of the South Mountain, and pushed his marauding parties as far as Waynesboro. On the twenty-second the remainder of Ewell's corps crossed the river and moved up the valley. They were followed on the twenty-fourth by Longstreet and Hill, who crossed at Williamsport and Shepherdstown, and, pushing up the valley, encamped at Chambersburg on the twenty-seventh. In this way the whole Rebel army, estimated at 90,000 infantry, upwards of 10,000 cavalry, and 4,000 or 5,000 artillery, making a total of 105,000 of all arms, was concentrated in Pennsylvania.

Up to this time no report of Hooker's movements had been received by General Lee, who, having been deprived of his cavalry, had no means of obtaining information. Rightly judging, however, that no time would be lost by the Union army in the pursuit, in order to detain it on the eastern side of the mountains in Maryland and Pennsylvania, and thus preserve his communications by the way of Williamsport, he had, before his own arrival at Chambersburg, directed Ewell to send detachments from his corps to Carlisle and York. The latter detachment, under Early, passed through this place on the twenty-sixth of June. You need not, fellow-citizens of Gettysburg, that I should recall to you those moments of alarm and distress, precursors as they were of the more trying scenes which were so soon to follow.

As soon as General Hooker perceived that the advance of the Confederates into the Cumberland valley was not a mere feint to draw him away from Washington, he moved rapidly in pursuit. Attempts, as we have seen, were made to harass and retard his passage across the Potomac. These attempts were not only altogether unsuccessful, but were so unskillfully made as to place the entire Federal army between the cavalry of Stuart and the army of Lee. While the latter was massed in the Cumberland valley, Stuart was east of the mountains, with Hooker's army between, and Gregg's Cavalry in close pursuit. Stuart was accordingly compelled to force a march northward, which was destitute of strategical character, and which deprived his chief of all means of obtaining intelligence.

Not a moment had been lost by General Hooker in the pursuit of Lee. The day after the Rebel army entered Maryland, the Union army crossed the Potomac at Edward's Ferry, and by the twenty-eighth of June lay between Harper's Ferry and Frederick. The force of the enemy on that day was partly at Chambersburg, and partly moving on the Cashtown road in the direction of Gettysburg, while the detachments from Ewell's corps, of which mention has been made, had reached the Susquehannah opposite Harrisburg and Columbia. That a great battle must soon be fought, no one could doubt; but in the apparent and perhaps real absence of plan on the part of Lee, it was impossible to foretell the precise scene of the encounter. Wherever fought, consequences the most momentous hung upon the result.

In this critical and anxious state of affairs, General Hooker was relieved, and General Meade was summoned to the chief command of the army. It appears to my unmilitary judgment to reflect the highest credit upon him, upon his predecessor, and upon the corps commanders of the Army of the Potomac, that a change could take place in the chief command of so large a force on the eve of a general battle,—the various corps necessarily moving on lines somewhat divergent, and all in ignorance of the enemy's intended point of concentration,—and that not an hour's hesitation should ensue in the advance of any portion of the entire army.

Having assumed the chief command on the twenty-eighth, General Meade directed his left wing, under Reynolds, upon Emmittsburg and his right upon New Windsor, leaving General French with 11,000 men to protect the Baltimore and Ohio Railroad, and convoy the public property from Harper's Ferry to Washington. Buford's cavalry was then at this place, and Kilpatrick's at Hanover, where he encountered and defeated the rear of Stuart's cavalry, who was roving the country in search of the main army of Lee. On the Rebel side, Hill had reached Fayetteville on the Cashtown road on the twenty-eighth, and was followed on the same road by Longstreet on the twenty-ninth. The eastern side of the mountain, as seen from Gettysburg, was lighted up at night by the camp-fires of the enemy's advance, and the country swarmed with his foraging parties. It was now too evident to be questioned, that the thunder-cloud, so long gathering blackness, would soon burst on some part of the devoted vicinity of Gettysburg.

The thirtieth of June was a day of important preparation. At half-past eleven o'clock in the morning, General Buford passed through Gettysburg, upon a reconnoissance in force, with his cavalry, upon the Chambersburg road. The information obtained by him was immediately communicated to General Reynolds, who was, in consequence, directed to occupy Gettysburg. That gallant officer accordingly, with the First Corps, marched from Emmittsburg to within six or seven miles of this place, and encamped on the right bank of Marsh's Creek. Our right wing, meantime, was moved to Manchester. On the same day the corps of Hill and Longstreet were pushed still farther forward on the Chambersburg road, and distributed in the vicinity of Marsh's Creek, while a reconnoissance was made by the Confederate General Pettigrew up to a very short distance from this place. Thus at nightfall on the thirtieth of June the greater part of the Rebel force was concentrated in the immediate vicinity of two corps of the Union army, the former refreshed by two days passed in comparative repose and deliberate preparation for the encounter, the latter separated by a march of one or two days from their supporting corps, and doubtful at what precise point they were to expect an attack.

And now the momentous day, a day to be forever remembered in the annals of the country, arrived. Early in the morning on the first of July the conflict began. I need not say that it would be impossible for me to comprise, within the limits of the hour, such a narrative as would do anything like full justice to the all-important events of these three great days, or to the merit of the brave officers and men of every rank, of every arm of the service, and of every loyal State, who bore their part in the tremendous struggle,—alike those who nobly sacrificed their lives for their country, and those who survive, many of them scarred with honorable wounds, the objects of our admiration and gratitude. The astonishingly minute, accurate, and graphic accounts contained in the journals of the day, prepared from personal observation by reporters, who witnessed the scenes and often shared the perils which they describe, and the highly valuable "Notes" of Professor Jacobs, of the University in this place, to which I am greatly indebted, will abundantly supply the deficiency of my necessarily too condensed statement.*

General Reynolds, on arriving at Gettysburg in the morning of the first, found Buford with his cavalry warmly engaged with the enemy, whom he held most gallantly

---

* Besides the sources of information mentioned in the text, I have been kindly favored with a memorandum of the operations of the three days drawn up for me by direction of Major-General Meade (anticipating the promulgation of his official report), by one of his aids, Colonel Theodore Lyman, from whom also I have received other important communications relative to the campaign. I have received very valuable documents relative to the battle from Major-General Halleck, Commander-in-Chief of the army, and have been much assisted in drawing up the sketch of the campaign, by the detailed reports, kindly transmitted to me in manuscript from the Adjutant-General's office, of the movements of every corps of the army, for each day, after the breaking up from Fredericksburg commenced. I have derived much assistance from Colonel John B. Bachelder's oral explanations of his beautiful and minute drawing (about to be engraved) of the field of the three days' struggle. With the information derived from these sources I have compared the statements in General Lee's official report of the campaign, dated 31st July, 1863, a well-written article, purporting to be an account of the three days' battle, in the *Richmond Enquirer* of the 22nd of July, and the article on "The Battle of Gettysburg and the Campaign of Pennsylvania," by an officer, apparently a colonel in the British army, in *Blackwood's Magazine* for September. The value of the information contained in this last essay may be seen by comparing the remark

in check. Hastening himself to the front, General Reynolds directed his men to be moved over the fields from the Emmittsburg road, in front of McMillan's and Dr. Schmucker's, under cover of the Seminary Ridge. Without a moment's hesitation, he attacked the enemy, at the same time sending orders to the Eleventh Corps (General Howard's) to advance as promptly as possible. General Reynolds immediately found himself engaged with a force which greatly outnumbered his own, and had scarcely made his dispositions for the action when he fell, mortally wounded, at the head of his advance. The command of the First Corps devolved on General Doubleday, and that of the field on General Howard, who arrived at 11.30 with Schurz's and Barlow's divisions of the Eleventh Corps, the latter of whom received a severe wound. Thus strengthened, the advantage of the battle was for some time on our side. The attacks of the Rebels were vigorously repulsed by Wadsworth's division of the First Corps, and a large number of prisoners, including General Archer, were captured. At length, however, the continued reinforcement of the Confederates from the main body in the neighborhood, and by the divisions of Rodes and Early, coming down by separate lines from Heidlersberg and taking post on our extreme right, turned the fortunes of the day. Our army, after contesting the ground for five hours, was obliged to yield to the enemy, whose force outnumbered them two to one; and toward the close of the afternoon General Howard deemed it prudent to withdraw the two corps to the heights where we are now assembled. The greater part of the First Corps passed through the outskirts of the town, and reached the hill without serious loss or molestation. The Eleventh Corps and portions of the First, not being aware that the enemy had already entered the town from the north, attempted to force their way through Washington and Baltimore streets,

---

under date 27th of June, that "private property is to be rigidly protected," with the statement in the next sentence but one, "that all the cattle and farm-horses having been seized by Ewell, farm labor had come to a complete stand-still." He also, under date of 4th July, speaks of Lee's retreat being encumbered by "Ewell's *immense train of plunder*." This writer informs us that, on the evening of the 4th of July, he heard "reports coming in from the different *Generals* that the enemy [Meade's army] was *retiring*, and had been doing so all day long." At a consultation at head-quarters on the sixth, between Generals Lee, Longstreet, Hill, and Wilcox, this writer was told by some one, whose name he prudently leaves in blank, that the army had no intention at present of retreating for good, and that some of the enemy's despatches had been intercepted, in which the following words occur: "The noble, but unfortunate Army of the Potomac has again been obliged to retreat before superior numbers!" He does not appear to be aware that, in recording these wretched expedients, resorted to in order to keep up the spirits of Lee's army, he furnishes the most complete refutation of his own account of its good condition. I much regret that General Meade's official report was not published in season to enable me to take full advantage of it, in preparing the brief sketch of the battles of the three days contained in this Address. It reached me but the morning before it was sent to the press.

which, in the crowd and confusion of the scene, they did with a heavy loss in prisoners.

General Howard was not unprepared for this turn in the fortunes of the day. He had in the course of the morning caused Cemetery Hill to be occupied by General Steinwehr, with the second division of the Eleventh Corps. About the time of the withdrawal of our troops to the hill, General Hancock arrived, having been sent by General Meade, on hearing of the death of Reynolds, to assume the command of the field till he himself could reach the front. In conjunction with General Howard, General Hancock immediately proceeded to post troops and to repel an attack on our right flank. This attack was feebly made and promptly repulsed. At nightfall, our troops on the hill, who had so gallantly sustained themselves during the toil and peril of the day, were cheered by the arrival of General Slocum with the Twelfth Corps, and of General Sickles with a part of the Third.

Such was the fortune of the first day, commencing with decided success to our arms, followed by a check, but ending in the occupation of this all-important position. To you, fellow-citizens of Gettysburg, I need not attempt to portray the anxieties of the ensuing night. Witnessing as you had done with sorrow the withdrawal of our army through your streets, with a considerable loss of prisoners,—mourning as you did over the brave men who had fallen,—shocked with the wide-spread desolation around you, of which the wanton burning of the Harman House had given the signal,—ignorant of the near approach of General Meade, you passed the weary hours of the night in painful expectation.

Long before the dawn of the second of July, the new Commander-in-Chief had reached the ever-memorable field of service and glory. Having received intelligence of the events in progress, and informed by the reports of Generals Hancock and Howard of the favorable character of the position, he determined to give battle to the enemy at this point. He accordingly directed the remaining corps of the army to concentrate at Gettysburg with all possible expedition, and breaking up his head quarters at Taneytown at 10 P. M., he arrived at the front at one o'clock in the morning of the second of July. Few were the moments given to sleep, during the rapid watches of that brief midsummer's night, by officers or men, though half of our troops were exhausted by the conflict of the day, and the residue wearied by the forced marches which had brought them to the rescue. The full moon, veiled by thin clouds, shone down that night on a strangely unwonted scene. The silence of the grave-yard was broken by the heavy tramp of armed men, by the neigh of the war-horse, the harsh rattle of the wheels of artillery hurrying to their stations, and all the indescribable tumult of preparation. The various corps of the army, as they arrived, were moved to their positions, on the spot where we are assembled, and the ridges that extend southeast and southwest; batteries were planted, and breastworks thrown up. The Second and Fifth Corps, with the rest of the Third, had reached the ground by seven o'clock, A. M.; but it was not till two o'clock in the afternoon that Sedgwick arrived with the Sixth Corps. He had marched thirty-four miles since nine o'clock on the evening before. It was only on his arrival that the Union army approached an equality of numbers with that of the Rebels, who were posted upon the opposite and parallel ridge, distant from a mile to a mile and a half, overlapping our position on either wing, and probably exceeding by ten thousand the army of General Meade.*

And here I cannot but remark on the providential inaction of the Rebel army. Had the contest been renewed by it at daylight on the second of July, with the First and Eleventh Corps exhausted by the battle and the retreat, the Third and Twelfth weary from their forced march, and the Second, Fifth and Sixth not yet arrived, nothing but a miracle could have saved the army from a great disaster. Instead of this, the day dawned, the sun rose, the cool hours of the morning passed, the forenoon and a considerable part of the afternoon wore away, without the slightest aggressive movement on the part of the enemy. Thus time was given for half of our forces to arrive and take their place in the lines, while the rest of the army enjoyed a much-needed half-day's repose.

At length, between three and four o'clock in the afternoon, the work of death began. A signal-gun from the hostile batteries was followed by a tremendous cannonade along the Rebel lines, and this by a heavy advance of infantry, brigade after brigade, commencing on the enemy's right against the left of our army, and so onward to the left centre. A forward movement of General Sickles, to gain a commanding position from which to repel the Rebel attack drew upon him a destructive fire from the enemy's batteries, and a furious assault from Longstreet's and Hill's advancing

---

* In the Address as originally prepared, judging from the best sources of information then within my reach, I assumed the equality of the two armies on the second and third of July. Subsequent inquiry has led me to think that I underrated somewhat the strength of Lee's force at Gettysburg, and I have corrected the text accordingly. General Halleck, however, in his official report accompanying the President's messages, states the armies to have been equal.

troops. After a brave resistance on the part of his corps, he was forced back, himself falling severely wounded. This was the critical moment of the second day ; but the Fifth and a part of the Sixth Corps, with portions of the First and Second, were promptly brought to the support of the Third. The struggle was fierce and murderous, but by sunset our success was decisive, and the enemy was driven back in confusion. The most important service was rendered toward the close of the day, in the memorable advance between Round Top and Little Round Top, by General Crawford's division of the Fifth Corps, consisting of two brigades of the Pennsylvania Reserves, of which one company was from this town and neighbourhood. The Rebel force was driven back with great loss in killed and prisoners. At eight o'clock in the evening a desperate attempt was made by the enemy to storm the position of the Eleventh Corps on Cemetery Hill ; but here, too, after a terrible conflict, he was repulsed with immense loss. Ewell, on our extreme right, which had been weakened by the withdrawal of the troops sent over to support our left, had succeeded in gaining a foothold within a portion of our lines, near Spangler's Spring. This was the only advantage obtained by the Rebels to compensate them for the disasters of the day, and of this, as we shall see, they were soon deprived.

Such was the result of the second act of this eventful drama,—a day hard fought and at one moment anxious, but, with the exception of the slight reverse just named, crowned with dearly earned but uniform success to our arms, auspicious of a glorious termination of the final struggle. On these good omens the night fell.

In the course of the night, General Geary returned to his position on the right, from which he had hastened the day before to strengthen the Third Corps. He immediately engaged the enemy, and, after a sharp and decisive action, drove them out of our lines, recovering the ground which had been lost on the preceding day. A spirited contest was kept up all the morning on this part of the line ; but General Geary, reinforced by Wheaton's brigade of the Sixth Corps, maintained his position, and inflicted very severe losses on the Rebels.

Such was the cheering commencement of the third day's work, and with it ended all serious attempts of the enemy on our right. As on the preceding day, his efforts were now mainly directed against our left centre and left wing. From eleven till half-past one o'clock, all was still,—a solemn pause of preparation, as if both armies were nerving themselves for the supreme effort. At length the awful silence, more terrible than the wildest tumult of battle, was broken by the roar of two hundred and fifty pieces of artillery from the opposite ridges, joining in a cannonade of unsurpassed violence,—the Rebel batteries along two-thirds of their line pouring their fire upon Cemetery Hill, and the centre and left wing of our army. Having attempted in this way for two hours, but without success, to shake the steadiness of our lines, the enemy rallied his forces for a last grand assault. Their attack was principally directed against the position of our Second Corps. Successive lines of Rebel infantry moved forward with equal spirit and steadiness from their cover on the wooded crest of Seminary Ridge, crossing the intervening plain, and, supported right and left by their choicest brigades, charged furiously up to our batteries. Our own brave troops of the Second Corps, supported by Doubleday's division and Stannard's brigade of the First, received the shock with firmness; the ground on both sides was long and fiercely contested, and was covered with the killed and the wounded; the tide of battle flowed and ebbed across the plain, till, after "a determined and gallant struggle," as it is pronounced by General Lee, the Rebel advance, consisting of two-thirds of Hill's corps and the whole of Longstreet's,—including Pickett's division, the *élite* of his corps, which had not yet been under fire, and was now depended upon to decide the fortune of this last eventful day,—was driven back with prodigious slaughter, discomfited and broken. While these events were in progress at our left centre, the enemy was driven, with a considerable loss of prisoners, from a strong position on our extreme left, from which he was annoying our force on Little Round Top. In the terrific assault on our centre, Generals Hancock and Gibbon were wounded. In the Rebel army, Generals Armistead, Kemper, Pettigrew, and Trimble were wounded, the first named mortally, the latter also made prisoner. General Garnett was killed, and thirty-five hundred officers and men made prisoners.

These were the expiring agonies of the three days' conflict, and with them the battle ceased. It was fought by the Union army with courage and skill, from the first cavalry skirmish on Wednesday morning to the fearful rout of the enemy on Friday afternoon, by every arm and every rank of the service, by officers and men, by cavalry, artillery and infantry. The superiority of numbers was with the enemy, who were led by the ablest commanders in their service; and if the Union force had the advantage of a strong position, the Confederates had that of choosing time and place, the prestige of former victories over the Army of the Potomac, and of the success of the first day. Victory does not always fall to the lot of those who deserve it; but that so decisive a triumph, under circumstances like these, was gained by our troops, I would ascribe, under Providence, to the spirit of exalted patriotism that animated them, and a consciousness that they were fighting in a righteous cause.

All hope of defeating our army, and securing what General Lee calls "the valuable results" of such an achievement, having vanished, he thought only of rescuing from destruction the remains of his shattered forces. In killed, wounded, and missing, he had, as far as can be ascertained, suffered a loss of about 37,000 men,—rather more than a third of the army with which he is supposed to have marched into Pennsylvania. Perceiving that his only safety was in rapid retreat, he commenced withdrawing his troops at daybreak on the fourth, throwing up field-works in front of our left, which, assuming the appearance of a new position, were intended probably to protect the rear of his army in their retreat. That day—sad celebration of the Fourth of July for an army of Americans—was passed by him in hurrying off his trains. By nightfall, the main army was in full retreat on the Cashtown and Fairfield roads, and it moved with such precipitation, that, short as the nights were, by daylight the following morning, notwithstanding a heavy rain, the rear-guard had left its position. The struggle of the last two days resembled in many respects the battle of Waterloo; and if, in the evening of the third day, General Meade, like the Duke of Wellington, had had the assistance of a powerful auxiliary army to take up the pursuit, the rout of the Rebels would have been as complete as that of Napoleon.

Owing to the circumstance just named, the intentions of the enemy were not apparent on the fourth. The moment his retreat was discovered, the following morning, he was pursued by our cavalry on the Cashton road, and through the Emmittsburg and Monterey passes, and by Sedgwick's corps on the Fairfield road. His rear-guard was briskly attacked at Fairfield; a great number of wagons and ambulances were captured in the passes of the mountains; the country swarmed with his stragglers, and his wounded were literally emptied from the vehicles containing them into the farm-houses on the road. General Lee, in his report, makes repeated mention of the Union prisoners whom he conveyed into Virginia, somewhat overstating their number. He states, also, that "such of his wounded as were in a condition to be removed" were forwarded to Williamsport. He does not mention that the number of his wounded *not* removed, and left to the Christian care of the victors, was 7,540, not one of whom failed of any attention which it was possible, under the circumstances of the case, to afford them, not one of whom, certainly, has been put upon Libby-prison fare,—lingering death by starvation. Heaven forbid, however, that we should claim any merit for the exercise of common humanity.

Under the protection of the mountain-ridge, whose narrow passes are easily held even by a retreating army, General Lee reached Williamsport in safety, and took up a strong position opposite to that place. General Meade necessarily pursued with the main army by a flank movement through Middletown. Turner's Pass having been secured by General French. Passing through the South Mountain, the Union army came up with that of the Rebels on the twelfth, and found it securely posted on the heights of Marsh Run. The position was reconnoitred, and preparations made for an attack on the thirteenth. The depth of the river, swollen by the recent rains, authorized the expectation that the enemy would be brought to a general engagement the following day. An advance was accordingly made by General Meade on the morning of the fourteenth; but it was soon found that the Rebels had escaped in the night, with such haste that Ewell's corps forded the river, where the water was breast high. The cavalry, which had rendered the most important services during the three days, and in harassing the enemy's retreat, was now sent in pursuit, and captured two guns and a large number of prisoners. In an action which took place at Falling Waters, General Pettigrew was mortally wounded. General Meade, in further pursuit of the Rebels, crossed the Potomac at Berlin. Thus again covering the approaches to Washington, he compelled the enemy to pass the Blue Ridge at one of the upper gaps; and in about six weeks from the commencement of the campaign, General Lee found himself again on the south side of the Rappahannock, with the probable loss of about a third part of his army.

Such, most inadequately recounted, is the history of the ever-memorable three days, and of the events immediately preceding and following. It has been pretended in order to diminish the magnitude of this disaster to the Rebel cause, that it was merely the repulse of an attack on a strongly defended position. The tremendous losses on both sides are a sufficient answer to this misrepresentation, and attest the courage and obstinacy with which the three days' battle was waged. Few of the great conflicts of modern times have cost victors and vanquished so great a sacrifice. On the Union side, there fell, in the whole campaign, of generals killed. Reynolds, Weed, and Zook, and wounded, Barlow, Barnes, Butterfield. Doubleday, Gibbon, Graham. Hancock. Sickles, and Warren; while of officers below the rank of general, and men, there were 2,834 killed, 13,709 wounded, and 6,643 missing. On the Confederate side, there were killed on the field or mortally wounded, Generals Armistead. Barksdale, Garnett, Pender, Pettigrew, and Semmes; and wounded, Heth, Hood. Johnson, Kemper, Kimball, and Trimble. Of officers below the rank of general, and men, there were taken prisoners, including the wounded, 13,621, an amount ascertained officially. Of the wounded in a condition to be removed, of the killed and the missing, the enemy has made no return. They are estimated from the best data which the nature of the case admits, at 23,000. General Meade also captured three cannon and forty-one standards ; and 24,978 small arms were collected on the battle field.

I must leave to others, who can do it from personal observation, to describe the mournful spectacle presented by these hill-sides and plains at the close of the terrible conflict. It was a saying of the Duke of Wellington, that next to a defeat, the saddest thing is a victory. The horrors of the battle field, after the contest is over, the sights and sounds of woe,—let me throw a pall over the scene, which no words can adequately depict to those who have not witnessed it, on which no one who has witnessed it, and who has a heart in his bosom, can bear to dwell. One drop of balm alone, one drop of heavenly, life-giving balm, mingles in this bitter cup of misery. Scarcely has the cannon ceased to roar, when the brethren and sisters of Christian benevolence, ministers of compassion, angels of pity, hasten to the field and the hospital, to moisten the parched tongue, to bind the ghastly wounds, to soothe the parting agonies alike of friend and foe, and to catch the last whispered messages of love from dying lips. " Carry this miniature back to my dear wife, but do not take it from my bosom till I am gone." " Tell my little sister not to grieve for me ; I am willing to die for my country." " Oh, that my mother were here !" When since Aaron stood between the living and the dead was there ever so gracious a ministry as this ? It has been said that it is characteristic of Americans to treat women with a deference not paid to them in any other country. I will not undertake to say whether this is so ; but I will say, that, since this terrible war has been waged, the women of the loyal States, if never before, have entitled themselves to our highest admiration and gratitude,—alike those who at home, often with fingers unused to the toil, often bowed beneath their own domestic cares, have performed an amount of daily labor not exceeded by those who work for their daily bread, and those who, in the hospitals and the tents of the Sanitary and Christian Commissions, have rendered services which millions could not buy. Happily, the labor and the service are their own reward. Thousands of matrons and thousands of maidens have experienced a delight in these homely toils and services, compared with which the pleasures of the ball-room and the opera-house are tame and unsatisfactory. This on earth is reward enough, but a richer is in store for them. Yes, brothers, sisters of charity, while you bind up the wounds of the poor sufferers,—the humblest, perhaps, that have shed their blood for the country,—forget not Who it is that will hereafter say to you, "Inasmuch as ye have done it unto one of the least of these my BRETHREN, ye have done it unto me."

And now, friends, fellow-citizens, as we stand among these honored graves, the momentous question presents itself, Which of the two parties to the war is responsible for all this suffering, for this dreadful sacrifice of life, the lawful and constitutional government of the United States, or the ambitious men who have rebelled against it? I say "rebelled" against it, although Earl Russell, the British Secretary of State for Foreign Affairs, in his recent temperate and conciliatory speech in Scotland, seems to intimate that no prejudice ought to attach to that word, inasmuch as our English forefathers rebelled against Charles I. and James II., and our American fathers rebelled against George III. These certainly are venerable precedents, but they prove only that it is just and proper to rebel against oppressive governments. They do not prove that it was just and proper for the son of James II. to rebel against George I., or his grandson Charles Edward to rebel against George II.; nor, as it seems to me, ought these dynastic struggles, little better than family quarrels, to be compared with this monstrous conspiracy against the American Union. These precedents do not prove that it was just and proper for the "disappointed great men" of the cotton-growing States to rebel against "the most beneficent government of which history gives us any account," as the Vice-President of the Confederacy, in November, 1860, charged them with doing. They do not create a presumption even in favor of the disloyal slaveholders of the South, who, living under a government of which Mr. Jefferson Davis, in the session of 1860–61, said that it was "the best government ever instituted by man, unexceptionably administered, and under which the people have been prosperous beyond comparison with any other people whose career has been recorded in history," rebelled against it because their aspiring politicians, himself among the rest, were in danger of losing their monopoly of its offices. What would have been thought by an impartial posterity of the American rebellion against George III., if the colonists had at all times been more than equally represented in parliament, and James Otis and Patrick Henry and Washington and Franklin and the Adamses and Hancock and Jefferson, and men of their stamp, had for two generations enjoyed the confidence of the sovereign and administered the government of the empire? What would have been thought of the rebellion against Charles I., if Cromwell and the men of his school had been the responsible advisers of that prince from his accession to the throne, and then, on account of a partial change in the ministry, had brought his head to the block, and involved the country in a desolating war, for the sake of dismembering it and establishing a new government south of the Trent? What would have been thought of the Whigs of 1688, if they had themselves composed the cabinet of James II., and been the advisers of the measures and the promoters of the policy which drove him into exile? The Puritans of 1640 and the Whigs of 1688 rebelled against arbitrary power in order to establish constitutional liberty. If they had risen against Charles and James because those monarchs favored equal rights, and in order themselves " for the first time in the history of the world" to establish an oligarchy "founded on the corner-stone of slavery," they would truly have furnished a precedent for the Rebels of the South, but their cause would not have been sustained by the eloquence of Pym or of Somers, nor sealed with the blood of Hampden or Russell.

I call the war which the Confederates are waging against the Union a "rebellion," because it is one, and in grave matters it is best to call things by their right names. I speak of it as a crime, because the Constitution of the United States so regards it, and puts "rebellion" on a par with "invasion." The constitution and law not only of England, but of every civilized country, regard them in the same light; or rather they consider the rebel in arms as far worse than the alien enemy. To levy war against the United States is the constitutional definition of treason, and that crime is by every civilized government regarded as the highest which citizen or subject can commit. Not content with the sanctions of human justice, of all the crimes against the law of the land it is singled out for its denunciations of religion. The litanies of every church in Christendom whose ritual embraces that office, as far as I am aware, from the metropolitan cathedrals of Europe to the humblest missionary chapel in the islands of the sea, concur with the Church of England in imploring the Sovereign of the universe, by the most awful adjurations which the heart of man can conceive or his tongue utter, to deliver us from "sedition, privy conspiracy, and rebellion." And reason good; for while a rebellion against tyranny,—a rebellion designed, after prostrating arbitrary power, to establish free government on the basis of justice and truth,—is an enterprise on which good men and angels may look with complacency, an unprovoked rebellion of ambitious men against a beneficent government, for the purpose—the avowed purpose—of establishing, extending, and perpetuating any form of injustice and wrong, is an imitation on earth of that first foul revolt of "the Infernal Serpent," against which the Supreme Majesty of heaven sent forth the armed myriads of his angels, and clothed the right arm of His Son with the three-bolted thunders of omnipotence.

Lord Bacon, in "the true marshalling of the sovereign degrees of honor," assigns the first place to "the *Conditores Imperiorum*, founders of States and Commonwealths;" and, truly, to build up from the discordant elements of our nature, the passions, the interests, and the opinions of the individual man, the rivalries of families, clan, and tribe, the influences of climate and geographical position, the accidents of peace and war accumulated for ages,—to build up from these oftentimes warring elements a well-compacted, prosperous, and powerful State, if it were to be accomplished by one effort or in one generation, would require a more than mortal skill. To contribute in some notable degree to this, the greatest work of man, by wise and patriotic counsel in peace and loyal heroism in war, is as high as human merit can well rise, and far more than to any of those to whom Bacon assigns this highest place of honor, whose names can hardly be repeated without a wondering smile,—Romulus, Cyrus, Cæsar, Ottoman, Ismael,—is it due to our Washington as the founder of the American Union. But if to achieve or help to achieve this greatest work of man's wisdom and virtue gives title to a place among the chief benefactors, rightful heirs of the benedictions of mankind, by equal reason shall the bold, bad men who seek to undo the noble work, *Eversores Imperiorum*, destroyers of States, who for base and selfish ends rebel against beneficent governments, seek to overturn wise constitutions, to lay powerful republican Unions at the foot of foreign thrones, to bring on civil and foreign war, anarchy at home, dictation abroad, desolation, ruin,—by equal reason, I say, yes, a thousandfold stronger, shall they inherit the execrations of the ages.

But to hide the deformity of the crime under the cloak of that sophistry which strives to make the worst appear the better reason, we are told by the leaders of the Rebellion that in our complex system of government the separate States are "sovereigns," and that the central power is only an "agency" established by these sovereigns to manage certain little affairs,—such, forsooth, as Peace, War, Army, Navy, Finance, Territory, and Relations with the native tribes,—which they could not so conveniently administer themselves. It happens, unfortunately for this theory, that the Federal Constitution (which has been adopted by the people of every State of the Union as much as their own State constitutions have been adopted, and is declared to be paramount to them) nowhere recognizes the States as "sovereigns,"—in fact, that, by their names, it does not recognize them at all; while the authority established by that instrument is recognized, in its text, not as an "agency," but as "the Government of the United States." By that Constitution, moreover, which purports in its preamble to be ordained and established by "the People of the United States," it is expressly provided that "the members of the State legislatures, and all executive and judicial officers, shall be bound by oath or affirmation to support the Constitution." Now it is a common thing, under all governments, for an agent to be bound by oath to be faithful to his sovereign; but I never heard before of sovereigns being bound by oath to be faithful to their agency.

Certainly I do not deny that the separate States are clothed with sovereign powers for the administration of local affairs. It is one of the most beautiful features of our mixed system of government; but it is equally true that, in adopting the Federal Constitution, the States abdicated, by express renunciation, all the most important functions of national sovereignty, and, by one comprehensive, self-denying clause, gave up all right to contravene the Constitution of the United States. Specifically, and by enumeration, they renounced all the most important prerogatives of independent States for peace and for war,—the right to keep troops or ships of war in time of peace, or to engage in war unless actually invaded; to enter into compact with another State or a foreign power; to lay any duty on tonnage, or any impost on exports or imports, without the consent of Congress; to enter into any treaty, alliance, or confederation; to grant letters of marque and reprisal, and to emit bills of credit,—while all these powers and many others are expressly vested in the General Government. To ascribe to political communities, thus limited in their jurisdiction,—who cannot even establish a post-office on their own soil,—the character of independent sovereignty, and to reduce a national organization, clothed with all the transcendent powers of government, to the name and condition of an "agency" of the States, proves nothing but that the logic of secession is on a par with its loyalty and patriotism.

Oh, but "the reserved rights!" And what of the reserved rights? The tenth amendment of the Constitution, supposed to provide for "reserved rights," is constantly misquoted. By that amendment, "the *powers* not delegated to the United

States by the Constitution, nor prohibited by it to the States, are reserved to the States respectively, or to the People." The "powers" reserved must of course be such as could have been, but were not delegated to the United States,—could have been, but were not prohibited to the States ; but to speak of the *right* of an *individual* State to secede, as a *power* that could have been, though it was not delegated to the *United States*, is simple nonsense.

But waiving this obvious absurdity, can it need a serious argument to prove that there can be no State right to enter into a new confederation reserved under a constitution which expressly prohibits a State to " enter into any treaty, alliance or confederation," or any " agreement or compact with another State or a foreign power !" To say that the State may, by enacting the preliminary farce of secession, acquire the right to do the prohibited things,—to say, for instance, that though the States, in forming the Constitution, delegated to the United States and prohibited to themselves the power of declaring war, there was by implication reserved to each State the right of seceding and then declaring war ; that, though they expressly prohibited to the States and delegated to the United States the entire treaty-making power, they reserved by implication (for an express reservation is not pretended) to the individual States, to Florida, for instance, the right to secede, and then to make a treaty with Spain retroceding that Spanish colony, and thus surrendering to a foreign power the key to the Gulf of Mexico,—to maintain propositions like these, with whatever affected seriousness it is done, appears to me egregious trifling.

Pardon me, my friends, for dwelling on these wretched sophistries. But it is these which conducted the armed hosts of rebellion to your doors on the terrible and glorious days of July, and which have brought upon the whole land the scourge of an aggressive and wicked war,—a war which can have no other termination compatible with the permanent safety and welfare of the country but the complete destruction of the military power of the enemy. I have, on other occasions, attempted to show that to yield to his demands and acknowledge his independence, thus resolving the Union at once into two hostile governments, with a certainty of further disintegration, would annihilate the strength and the influence of the country as a member of the family of nations ; afford to foreign powers the opportunity and the temptation for humiliating and disastrous interference in our affairs ; wrest from the Middle and Western States some of their great natural outlets to the sea and of their most important lines of internal communication ; deprive the commerce and navigation of the country of two-thirds of our sea-coast and of the fortresses which protect it; not only so, but would enable each individual State,—some of them with a white population equal to a good-sized Northern county,—or rather the dominant party in each State, to cede its territory, its harbors, its fortresses, the mouths of its rivers, to any foreign power. It cannot be that the people of the loyal States,—that twenty-two millions of brave and prosperous freemen,—will, for the temptation of a brief truce in an eternal border-war, consent to this hideous national suicide.

Do not think that I exaggerate the consequences of yielding to the demands of the leaders of the Rebellion. I understate them. They require of us not only all the sacrifices I have named, not only the cession to them, a foreign and hostile power, of all the territory of the United States at present occupied by the Rebel forces, but the abandonment to them of the vast regions we have rescued from their grasp,—of Maryland, of a part of Eastern Virginia and the whole of Western Virginia; the sea-coast of North and South Carolina, Georgia and Florida; Kentucky, Tennessee and Missouri; Arkansas, and the larger portion of Mississippi, Louisiana and Texas, —in most of which, with the exception of lawless guerillas, there is not a rebel in arms, in all of which the great majority of the people are loyal to the Union. We must give back, too, the helpless colored population, thousands of whom are perilling their lives in the ranks of our armies, to a bondage rendered tenfold more bitter by the momentary enjoyment of freedom. Finally, we must surrender every man in the Southern country, white or black, who has moved a finger or spoken a word for the restoration of the Union, to a reign of terror as remorseless as that of Robespierre, which has been the chief instrument by which the Rebellion has been organized and sustained, and which has already filled the prisons of the South with noble men, whose only crime is that they are not the worst of criminals. The South is full of such men. I do not believe there has been a day since the election of President Lincoln, when, if an ordinance of secession could have been fairly submitted, after a free discussion, to the mass of the people in any single Southern State, a majority of ballots would have been given in its favor. No, not in South Carolina. It is not possible that the majority of the people, even of that State, if permitted, without fear or favor, to give a ballot on the question, would have abandoned a leader like Petigru, and all the memories of the Gadsdens, the Rutledges, and the Cotesworth Pinckneys of the revolutionary and constitutional age, to follow the agitators of the present day.

Nor must we be deterred from the vigorous prosecution of the war by the suggestions, continually thrown out by the Rebels and those who sympathize with them, that, however it might have been at an earlier stage, there has been engendered by the operations of the war a state of exasperation and bitterness, which, independent of all reference to the original nature of the matters in controversy, will forever prevent the restoration of the Union, and the return of harmony between the two great sections of the country. This opinion I take to be entirely without foundation.

No man can deplore more than I do the miseries of every kind unavoidably incident to war. Who could stand on this spot and call to mind the scenes of the first days of July with any other feeling? A sad foreboding of what would ensue, if war should break out between North and South, has haunted me through life, and led me, perhaps too long, to tread in the path of hopeless compromise, in the fond endeavor to conciliate those who were predetermined not to be conciliated. But it is not true, as is pretended by the Rebels and their sympathizers, that the war has been carried on by the United States without entire regard to those temperaments which are enjoined by the law of nations, by our modern civilization, and by the spirit of Christianity. It would be quite easy to point out, in the recent military history of the leading European powers, acts of violence and cruelty, in the prosecution of their wars, to which no parallel can be found among us. In fact, when we consider the peculiar bitterness with which civil wars are almost invariably waged, we may justly boast of the manner in which the United States have carried on the contest. It is of course impossible to prevent the lawless acts of stragglers and deserters, or the occasional unwarrantable proceedings of subordinates on distant stations; but I do not believe there is, in all history, the record of a civil war of such gigantic dimensions where so little has been done in the spirit of vindictiveness as in this war, by the Government and the commanders of the United States; and this notwithstanding the provocation given by the Rebel Government by assuming the responsibility of wretches like Quantrell, refusing quarter to colored troops and scourging and selling into slavery free colored men from the North who fall into their hands, by covering the sea with pirates, refusing a just exchange of prisoners, while they crowd their armies with paroled prisoners not exchanged, and starving prisoners of war to death.

In the next place, if there are any present who believe that, in addition to the effect of the military operations of the war, the confiscation acts and emancipation proclamations have embittered the Rebels beyond the possibility of reconciliation,

I would request them to reflect that the tone of the Rebel leaders and Rebel press was just as bitter in the first months of the war, nay, before a gun was fired, as it is now. There were speeches made in Congress in the very last session before the outbreak of the Rebellion, so ferocious as to show that their authors were under the influence of a real frenzy. At the present day, if there is any discrimination made by the Confederate press in the affected scorn, hatred, and contumely with which every shade of opinion and sentiment in the loyal States is treated, the bitterest contempt is bestowed upon those at the North who still speak the language of compromise, and who condemn those measures of the administration which are alleged to have rendered the return of peace hopeless.

No, my friends, that gracious Providence which overrules all things for the best "from seeming evil still educing good," has so constituted our natures, that the violent excitement of the passions in one direction is generally followed by a reaction in an opposite direction, and the sooner for the violence. If it were not so,—if injuries inflicted and retaliated of necessity led to new retaliations, with forever accumulating compound interest of revenge, then the world, thousands of years ago, would have been turned into an earthly hell, and the nations of the earth would have been resolved into clans of furies and demons, each forever warring with his neighbor. But it is not so; all history teaches a different lesson. The Wars of the Roses in England lasted an entire generation, from the Battle of St. Albans in 1455, to that of Bosworth Field in 1485. Speaking of the former, Hume says: "This was the first blood spilt in that fatal quarrel, which was not finished in less than a course of thirty years; which was signalized by twelve pitched battles; which opened a scene of extraordinary fierceness and cruelty; is computed to have cost the lives of eighty princes of the blood; and almost entirely annihilated the ancient nobility of England. The strong attachments which, at that time, men of the same kindred bore to each other, and the vindictive spirit which was considered a point of honor, rendered the great families implacable in their resentments, and widened every moment the breech between the parties." Such was the state of things in England under which an entire generation grew up; but when Henry VII., in whom the titles of the two Houses were united, went up to London after the Battle of Bosworth Field, to mount the throne, he was everywhere received with joyous acclamations, "as one ordained and sent from heaven to put an end to the dissensions" which had so long afflicted the country.

The great Rebellion in England of the seventeenth century, after long and angry premonitions, may be said to have begun with the calling of the Long Parliament in 1640, and to have ended with the return of Charles II. in 1660,—twenty years of discord, conflict and civil war; of confiscation, plunder, havoc; a proud hereditary peerage trampled in the dust; a national church overturned, its clergy beggared, its most eminent prelate put to death; a military despotism established on the ruins of a monarchy which had subsisted seven hundred years, and the legitimate sovereign brought to the block; the great families which adhered to the king proscribed, impoverished, ruined; prisoners of war—a fate worse than starvation in Libby—sold to slavery in the West Indies; in a word, everything that can embitter and madden contending factions. Such was the state of things for twenty years; and yet, by no gentle transition, but suddenly, and "when the restoration of affairs appeared most hopeless," the son of the beheaded sovereign was brought back to his father's blood-stained throne, with such "unexpressible and universal joy" as led the merry monarch to exclaim "he doubted it had been his own fault he had been absent so long, for he saw nobody who did not protest he had ever wished for his return." "In this wonderful manner," says Clarendon, "and with this incredible expedition, did God put an end to a rebellion that had raged near twenty years, and had been carried on with all the horrid circumstances of murder, devastation and parricide, that fire and sword, in the hands of the most wicked men in the world"— it is a Royalist that is speaking—" could be instruments of, almost to the desolation of two kingdoms, and the exceeding defacing and deforming of the third. . . . By these remarkable steps did the merciful hand of God, in this short space of time, not only bind up and heal all those wounds, but even made the scar as undiscernable as, in respect of the deepness, was possible, which was a glorious addition to the deliverance."

In Germany, the wars of the Reformation and of Charles V. in the sixteenth century, the Thirty Years' War in the seventeenth century, the Seven Years' War in the eighteenth century, not to speak of other less celebrated contests, entailed upon that country all the miseries of intestine strife for more than three centuries. At the close of the last-named war,—which was the shortest of all and waged in the most civilized age,—" an officer," says Archenholz, "rode through seven villages in Hesse, and found in them but one human being." More than three hundred principalities, comprehended in the Empire, fermented with the fierce passions of proud and petty States; at the commencement of this period the castles of robber counts frowned upon every hill-top; a dreadful secret tribunal, whose seat no one knew, whose power none could escape, froze the hearts of men with terror throughout the land; religious hatred mingled its bitter poison in the seething caldron of provincial animosity: but of all these deadly enmities between the States of Germany scarcely the memory remains. There are controversies in that country at the present day, but they grow mainly out of the rivalry of the two leading powers. There is no country in the world in which the sentiment of national brotherhood is stronger.

In Italy, on the breaking up of the Roman Empire, society might be said to be resolved into its original elements,—into hostile atoms, whose only movement was that of mutual repulsion. Ruthless barbarians had destroyed the old organizations and covered the land with a merciless feudalism. As the new civilization grew up, under the wing of the Church, the noble families and the walled towns fell madly into conflict with each other; the secular feud of Pope and Emperor scourged the land; province against province, city against city, street against street, waged remorseless war with each other from father to son, till Dante was able to fill his imaginary hell with the real demons of Italian history. So ferocious had the factions become, that the great poet-exile himself, the glory of his native city and of his native language, was, by a decree of the municipality, condemned to be burned alive if found in the city of Florence. But these deadly feuds and hatreds yielded to political influences, as the hostile cities were grouped into States under stable governments; the lingering traditions of the ancient animosities gradually died away, and now Tuscan and Lombard, Sardinian and Neapolitan, as if to shame the degenerate sons of America, are joining in one cry for a united Italy.

In France, not to go back to the civil wars of the League in the sixteenth century and of the Fronde in the seventeenth; not to speak of the dreadful scenes throughout the kingdom, which followed the revocation of the edict of Nantes; we have, in the great revolution which commenced at the close of the last century, seen the blood-hounds of civil strife let loose as rarely before in the history of the world. The reign of terror established at Paris stretched its bloody Briarean arms to every city and village in the land, and if the most deadly feuds which ever divided a people had the power to cause permanent alienation and hatred, this surely was the occasion. But far otherwise the fact. In seven years from the fall of Robespierre, the strong arm of the youthful conqueror brought order out of this chaos of crime and woe; Jacobins, whose hands were scarcely cleansed from the best blood of France, met the returning emigrants, whose estates they had confiscated and whose kindred they had dragged to the guillotine, in the Imperial antechambers; and when, after another turn of the wheel of fortune, Louis XVIII. was restored to his throne, he took the regicide Fouché, who had voted for his brother's death, to his cabinet and confidence.

The people of loyal America will never ask you, Sir, to take to your confidence or admit again to a share in the government the hard-hearted men whose cruel lust of power has brought this desolating war upon the land, but there is no personal bitterness felt even against them. They may live, if they can bear to live after wantonly causing the death of so many thousands of their fellow-men; they may live in safe obscurity beneath the shelter of the government they have sought to overthrow, or they may fly to the protection of the governments of Europe,—some of them are already there, seeking, happily in vain, to obtain the aid of foreign powers in furtherance of their own treason. There let them stay. The humblest dead soldier, that lies cold and stiff in his grave before us, is an object of envy beneath the clods that cover him, in comparison with the living man, I care not with what trumpery credentials he may be furnished, who is willing to grovel at the foot of a foreign throne for assistance in compassing the ruin of his country.

But the hour is coming and now is, when the power of the leaders of the Rebellion to delude and inflame must cease. There is no bitterness on the part of the masses. The people of the South are not going to wage an eternal war, for the wretched pretexts by which this rebellion is sought to be justified. The bonds that unite us one People,—a substantial community of origin, language, belief and law (the four great ties that hold the societies of men together); common national and political interests; a common history; a common pride in a glorious ancestry; a common interest in this great heritage of blessings; the very geographical features of the country; the mighty rivers that cross the lines of climate and thus facilitate the interchange of natural and industrial products, while the wonder-working arm of the engineer has levelled the mountain-walls which separate the East and West, compelling your own Alleghanies, my Maryland and Pennsylvanian friends, to open wide their everlasting doors to the chariot wheels of traffic and travel,—these bonds of union are of perennial force and energy, while the causes of alienation are imaginary, factitious and transient. The heart of the People, North and South, is for the Union. Indications, too plain to be mistaken, announce the fact, both in the East and the West of the States in rebellion. In North Carolina and Arkansas the fatal charm at length is broken. At Raleigh and Little Rock the lips of honest and brave men are unsealed, and an independent press is unlimbering its artillery. When its rifled cannon shall begin to roar, the hosts of treasonable sophistry,—the mad delusions of the day,—will fly like the Rebel army through the passes of yonder mountain. The weary masses of the people are yearning to see the dear old flag again floating upon their capitols, and they sigh for the return of the peace, prosperity, and happiness, which they enjoyed under a government whose power was felt only in its blessings.

And now friends, fellow-citizens of Gettysburg and Pennsylvania, and you from remoter States, let me again, as we part, invoke your benediction on these honored graves. You feel, though the occasion is mournful, that it is good to be here. You feel that it was greatly auspicious for the cause of the country, that the men of the East and the men of the West, the men of nineteen sister States, stood side by side, on the perilous ridges of the battle. You now feel it a new bond of union, that they shall lie side by side, till a clarion, louder than that which marshalled them to the combat, shall awake their slumbers. God bless the Union;—it is dearer to us for the blood of brave men which has been shed in its defence. The spots on which they stood and fell; these pleasant heights; the fertile plain beneath them; the thriving village whose streets so lately rang with the strange din of war; the fields beyond the ridge, where the noble Reynolds held the advancing foe at bay, and, while he gave up his own life, assured, by his forethought and self-sacrifice, the triumph of the two succeeding days; the little streams which wind through the hills, on whose banks in after-times the wondering ploughman will turn up, with the rude weapons of savage warfare, the fearful missiles of modern artillery; Seminary Ridge, the Peach-Orchard, Cemetery, Culp, and Wolf Hill, Round Top, Little Round Top, humble names, henceforward dear and famous,—no lapse of time, no distance of space, shall cause you to be forgotten. "The whole earth," said Pericles, as he stood over the remains of his fellow-citizens, who had fallen in the first year of the Peloponnesian War, "the whole earth is the sepulchre of illustrious men." All time, he might have added, is the millennium of their glory. Surely I would do no injustice to the other noble achievements of the war, which have reflected such honor on both arms of the service, and have entitled the armies and the navy of the United States,

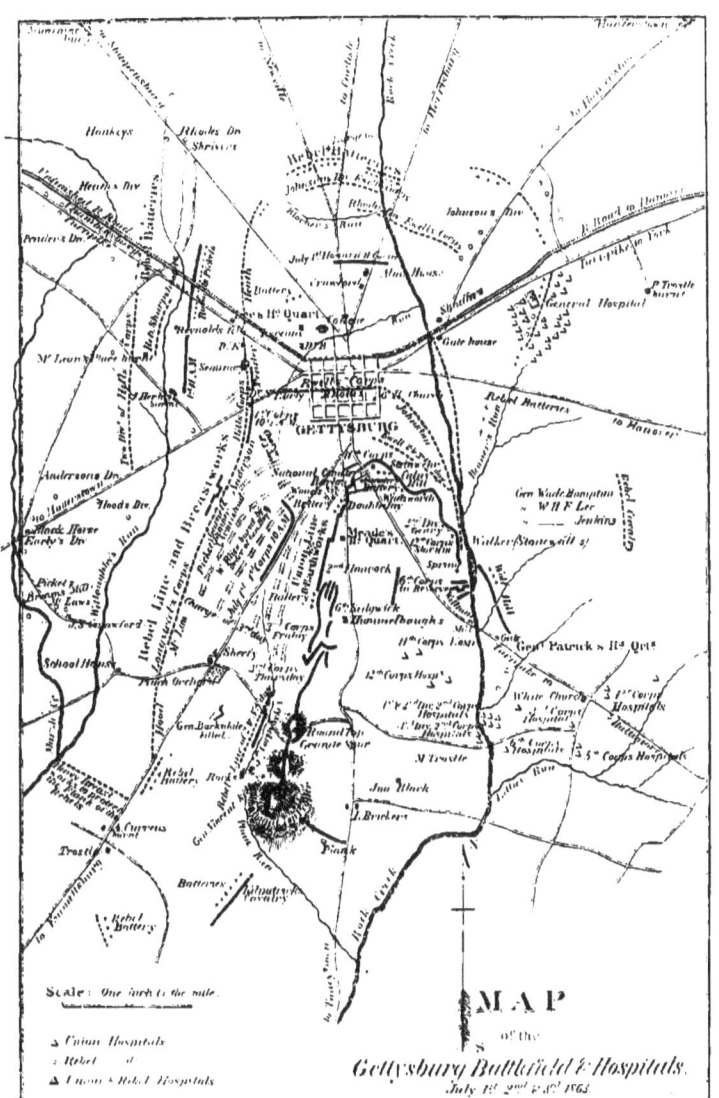

their officers and men, to the warmest thanks and the richest rewards which a grateful people can pay. But they, I am sure, will join us in saying, as we bid farewell to the dust of these martyr-heroes, that wheresoever throughout the civilized world the accounts of this great warfare are read, and down to the latest period of recorded time, in the glorious annals of our common country there will be no brighter page than that which relates to THE BATTLE OF GETTYSBURG.

8

HYMN COMPOSED BY B. B. FRENCH, ESQ., AT GETTYSBURG.

'Tis holy ground, –
This spot, where, in their graves,
We place our country's braves,
Who fell in Freedom's holy cause,
Fighting for liberties and laws ;
    Let tears abound.

    Here let them rest ;
And summer's heat and winter's cold
Shall glow and freeze above this mould,—
A thousand years shall pass away,—
A nation still shall mourn this clay,
    Which now is blest.

    Here, where they fell,
Oft shall the widow's tears be shed ;
Oft shall fond parents mourn their dead ;
The orphan here shall kneel and weep ;
And maidens, where their lovers sleep,
    Their woes shall tell.

    Great God in heaven !
Shall all this sacred blood be shed ?
Shall we thus mourn our glorious dead ?
Oh, shall the end be wrath and woe,
The knell of Freedom's overthrow,
    A country riven ?

    It will not be !
We trust, O God, Thy gracious power
To aid us in our darkest hour.
This be our prayer,—O Father ! save
A people's freedom from its grave.
    All praise to Thee !

DEDICATORY ADDRESS OF PRESIDENT LINCOLN.

Fourscore and seven years ago our fathers brought forth upon this continent a new nation, conceived in Liberty, and dedicated to the proposition that all men are created equal.

Now we are engaged in a great civil war, testing whether that nation, or any nation so conceived and so dedicated, can long endure. We are met on a great battle-field of that war. We are met to dedicate a portion of it, as the final resting-place of those who here gave their lives that that nation might live. It is altogether fitting and proper that we should do this.

But in a larger sense we cannot dedicate, we cannot consecrate, we cannot hallow this ground. The brave men, living and dead, who struggled here, have consecrated it far above our power to add or detract. The world will little note nor long remember what we say here, but it can never forget what they did here. It is for us, the living, rather to be dedicated here to the unfinished work that they have thus far so nobly carried on. It is rather for us to be here dedicated to the great task remaining before us,—that from these honored dead we take increased devotion to the cause for which they here gave the last full measure of devotion,—that we here highly resolve that the dead shall not have died in vain; that the nation shall, under God, have a new birth of freedom, and that the government of the people, by the people, and for the people, shall not perish from the earth.

DIRGE SUNG AT THE CONSECRATION OF THE SOLDIERS' CEMETERY.

WRITTEN BY JAS. G. PERCIVAL.

Oh, it is great for our country to die! whose ranks are contending;
  Bright is the wreath of our fame; glory awaits us for aye;
Glory, that never is dim, shining on with a light never ending;
  Glory, that never shall fade, never, oh never away!

Oh, it is sweet for our country to die! how softly reposes
  Warrior youth on his bier! wet by the tears of his love,—
Wet by a mother's warm tears; they crown him with garlands of roses;
  Weep, and then joyously turn,—bright where he triumphs above!

Not in Elysian fields, by the still oblivious river,
  Not in the Isles of the blest, over the blue rolling sea,
But on Olympian heights shall dwell the devoted for ever;
  There shall assemble the good, there the wise, valiant and free.

Oh, then how great for our country to die, in the front rank to perish!
  Firm with our breast to the foe, victory's shout in our ears!
Long they our statues shall crown, in songs our memory cherish;
  We shall look forth from our heaven, pleased the sweet music to hear.

The Benediction was pronounced by the Rev. H. L. Baugher, D. D., President of Pennsylvania College, Gettysburg.

EXERCISES

AT THE

Laying of the Corner Stone of the Monument

IN THE

SOLDIERS' NATIONAL CEMETERY AT GETTYSBURG.

JULY 4TH, 1865.

Laying of the Corner-Stone of the Monument.

THE PRESIDENT'S LETTER.

HIS Excellency, Andrew Johnson, President of the United States, having been prevented from being present, by reason of severe illness, sent the Marshal of the District of Columbia, Judge Gooding, as his special messenger, who presented the following communication from His Excellency:

EXECUTIVE MANSION, WASHINGTON, D. C., *July 3rd*, 1865.

MR. DAVID WILLS, *Chairman, etc., Gettysburg, Pa.*

DEAR SIR,—I had promised myself the pleasure of participating in person in the proceedings at Gettysburg to-morrow. That pleasure, owing to my indisposition, I am reluctantly compelled to forego. I should have been pleased, standing on that twice consecrated spot, to share with you your joy at the return of peace, to greet with you the surviving heroes of the war who come back with light hearts, though heavy laden with honors, and with you to drop grateful tears to the memory of those who will never return.

Unable to do so in person, I can only send you my greetings, and assure you of my full sympathy with the purpose and spirit of your exercises to-morrow. Of all the anniversaries of the Declaration of Independence, none has been more important and significant than that upon which you assemble.

Four years of struggle for our nation's life have been crowned with success; armed treason is swept from the land; our ports are re-opened; our relations with other nations are of the most satisfactory character; our internal commerce is free; our soldiers and sailors resume the peaceful pursuits of civil life; our flag floats in every breeze; and the only barrier to our national progress—human slavery—is for ever at an end. Let us trust that each recurring Fourth of July shall find our nation stronger in numbers, stronger in wealth, stronger in the harmony of its citizens, stronger in its devotion to nationality and freedom.

As I have often said, I believe that God sent this people on a mission among the nations of the earth, and that when He founded our nation He founded it in perpetuity. That faith sustained me through the struggle that is past. It sustains me now that new duties are devolved upon me and new dangers threaten us. I feel that whatever the means He uses, the Almighty is determined to preserve us as a people.

And since I know the love our fellow-citizens bear their country, and the sacrifices they have made for it, my abiding faith has become stronger than ever that a " government of the people " is the strongest as well as the best of governments.

In your joy to-morrow, I trust you will not forget the thousands of whites, as well as blacks, whom the war has emancipated, who will hail this Fourth of July with a delight which no previous Declaration of Independence ever gave them. Controlled so long by ambitious, selfish leaders, who used them for their own unworthy ends, they are now free to serve and cherish the government against whose life they, in their blindness, struck. I am greatly mistaken if in the States lately in rebellion we do not henceforward have an exhibition of such loyalty and patriotism as were never seen nor felt there before.

Having consecrated a National Cemetery, you are now to lay the corner-stone of a National Monument, which, in all human probability, will rise to the full height and proportion you design. Noble as this monument of stone may be, it will be but a faint symbol of the grand monument which, if we do our duty, we shall raise among the nations of the earth upon the foundation laid nine and eighty years ago in Philadelphia. Time shall wear away and crumble this monument, but that, based as it is, upon the consent, virtue, patriotism and intelligence of the people, each year shall make firmer and more imposing.

Your friend and fellow-citizen,

ANDREW JOHNSON.

Remarks and Prayer were made by the Rev. Stephen H. Tyng, D. D.

THE GETTYSBURG MONUMENTAL ODE.

(Sung by the National Union Musical Association.)

This battle field—our nation's glory,—
  Where sweetly sleeps our fallen braves ;
Proclaims aloud the tragic story—
  The story of their hallowed graves !

Yes ! here on Gettysburg's sad plain,
  This monument the tale will tell,
That thousands for their flag were slain—
  Whilst fighting for the Union—fell !

Here red artillery's deadly fire
  Mowed squadrons down in dread array ;
Here Meade compelled Lee to retire ;
  And Howard held his ground that day.

Then let those tattered banners wave ;
  For ever sacred be this ground ;
Sing pæans to those warriors brave,
  And be their deeds with glory crowned.

Wives, mothers, sisters, orphans dear,
  Shall gather round each clay-cold bed,
And mourn their loved ones buried here—
  Their husbands, fathers, brothers dead.

Now on this consecrated ground,
  Baptized with patriots' sacred blood,
We dedicate each glorious mound
  To the *Union Battle Flag and God!*

ORATION OF MAJOR-GENERAL O. O. HOWARD.

As I stand here to-day before a peaceful audience, composed as it is of beautiful ladies, joyous children and happy citizens, and think of my last visit to this place two years ago, and of the terrible scenes in which it was my lot to bear a part, I cannot help exclaiming, "How changed! how changed!" It is the same rich landscape, broad and beautiful, covered with every variety of natural objects to please the eye; the same wooded ridges and cultivated fields; the same neat little town clinging to the hill-side; the same broad avenues of approach; the same ravines and creeks—but, thank God! the awful magnificence of hosts arrayed against each other in deadly strife is wanting. Yonder heights are no longer crowned with hostile cannon; the valleys do not reverberate with their fearful roar; the groves and the houses do not give back the indescribable peal of the musketry fire. And oh, how like a dream, to-day seems that sad spectacle of broken tombstones, prostrate fences, and the ground strewn with our wounded and dead companions! Then follows, after battle, the mingling of friends and enemies, with suffering depicted in all possible modes of portraiture. The surgeons, with resolute hearts and bloody hands; the pale faces of relatives searching for dear ones; the busy sanitary and Christian workers—all pass before my mind in group after group.

My friends, my companions, my countrymen, suffer me to congratulate you anew to-day, this Fourth day of July, 1865, that this sad work is completely done, and that sweet peace has really dawned upon us.

On the nineteenth of November, 1863, this National Cemetery, a pious tribute to manliness and virtue, was consecrated. The Hon. Edward Everett delivered an address in his own rich, clear, elegant style, which, having been published, has long ago become historical, and affords us a complete and graphic account of the campaign and battle of Gettysburg. I am deeply grateful to this noble patriot for his indefatigable industry in securing facts, and for the clear narrative he has left us of this battle, in which every living loyal soldier who fought here, is now proud to have borne a part. He, joining the patriotic band of those that are honored by his eloquence, has gone to his reward; and let his memory ever be mingled with those here, upon whose graves he so earnestly invoked your benediction.

Mr. Everett was followed by the few remarkable words of President Lincoln. While Mr. Lincoln's name is so near and dear to us, and the memory of his work and sacrifice so fresh, I deem it not inappropriate to repeat his own words:

"Fourscore and seven years ago, our fathers brought forth upon this continent a new nation, conceived in liberty, and dedicated to the proposition that all men are created equal.

"Now we are engaged in a great civil war, testing whether that nation, or any nation, so conceived and so dedicated, can long endure. We are met on a great battle field of that war. We are met to dedicate a portion of it as the final resting-place of those who here gave their lives that that nation might live. It is altogether fitting and proper that we should do this.

"But in a larger sense we cannot dedicate, we cannot consecrate, we cannot hallow this ground. The brave men, living and dead, who struggled here, have consecrated it far above our power to add or detract. The world will little note, nor long remember, what we say here, but it can never forget what they did here. It is for us, the living, rather to be dedicated here to the unfinished work that they have thus far so nobly carried on. It is rather for us to be here dedicated to the great task remaining before us; that from these honored dead we take increased devotion to the cause for which they here gave the last full measure of devotion; that we here highly resolve that the dead shall not have died in vain; that the nation shall, under God, have a new birth of freedom, and that the government of the people, by the people, and for the people, shall not perish from the earth."

The civil war is ended; the test was complete. He, Abraham Lincoln, never forgot his own dedication till the work was finished. He did display even increased devotion if it were possible. The dead did not die in vain, and the nation has experienced already the new birth of freedom of which he spoke. Oh that in the last throes of darkness and crime God had seen it good to have spared us that great heart, out of which proceeded such welcome words of truth and encouragement! How very much of grateful recollection clusters around the name of Abraham Lincoln, as we pronounce it here among the dead who have died that their nation might not perish from the earth!

These grounds have already been consecrated, and are doubly sacred from the memory of our brethren who lie here, and from the association with those remarkable men, Mr. Everett and Mr. Lincoln, who gave tone to the exercises of consecration two years ago, whose own bodies are now resting beneath the sod, but whose spirit is still living, and unmistakably animating every true American heart this day. We have now been called to lay the corner-stone of a monument. This monument is not a mere family *record*, not the simple *memorial* of individual fame, nor the silent tribute to genius. It is raised to the soldier. It is a memorial of his life and his noble death. It embraces a patriotic brotherhood of heroes in its inscriptions, and is an unceasing herald of labor, suffering, union, liberty, and sacrifice. Let us then, as is proper on such an occasion as this, give a few thoughts to the American soldier.

We have now embraced under this generic name of soldier, the dutiful officer, the volunteer soldier, the regular, the colored and the conscript; but in my remarks I will present you the *private volunteer* as the representative American soldier.

In the early part of 1861, the true citizen heard that traitors at Washington had formed a conspiracy to overthrow the Government, and soon after, that the stars and stripes had been fired upon and had been hauled down at the bidding of an armed enemy in South Carolina; that the Capitol of the nation was threatened, and that our new President had called for help. How quickly the citizen answered the call! Almost like magic he sprang forth a soldier. His farm or his bench, his desk or his counter, was left behind, and you find him marching through the then gloomy, flagless, defiant streets of Baltimore, fully equipped for service, with uniform grey, blue, red or green—it then mattered not; with knapsack, cartridge-box, musket and bayonet, his outfit was all that was required. He was a little awkward, his accoutrements much awry, his will unsubdued. He did not keep step to music, nor always lock step with his companions. He had scarcely ever fired a musket, but he had become a soldier, put on the soldier's garb, set his face towards the enemy, and, God willing, he purposed never to turn back till the soldier's work was done. You meet him at Washington—on Meridian Hill perhaps; discipline and drill seize upon him, restrain his liberty and mould his body. Colonels, captains, lieutenants and sergeants, his former equals, order him about, and he must obey them. Oh what days! and oh what nights! Where is home and affection? Where is the soft bed and the loaded table? Change of climate, change of food, want of rest, want of all kinds of old things, and an influx of all sorts of new things, make him sick—yes, really sick in body and soul. But, in spite of a few doses of quinine and a wholesome hospital bed and diet (as the soldier of 1861 remembers them), his vigorous constitution and indomitable heart prevail, so that he is soon able to cross the Long Bridge and invade the sacred red clay of Virginia, with his companions in arms. Yet, perhaps, should you now observe him very closely, you will perceive his enthusiasm increasing faster even than his strength. He is on the enemy's side of the river ; now for strict guard duty ; now for the lonely picket amid the thickets, where men are killed by ambushed foes. How the eye and the ear, and, may I say it, the heart are quickened in these new and trying vigils! Before long, however, the soldier is inured to these things; be becomes familiar with every stump, tree, and pathway of approach, and his trusty gun, and stouter heart, defy any secret foe.

Presently you find him on the road to battle ; the hot weather of July, the usual load, the superadded twenty extra rounds of cartridges, and three days rations strung to his neck, and the long weary march, quite exhaust his strength during the very first day. He aches to leave the ranks and rest, but no, no! He did not leave home for the ignominious name of "straggler" and "skulker." Cost what it may, he toils on. The Acotink, the Cub Run, the never-to-be-forgotten Bull Run, are passed. Here, of a sudden, strange and terrible sounds strike upon his ear, and bear down upon his heart ; the booming of shotted cannon ; the screeching of bursted shell through the heated air, and the zip, zip, zip, of smaller balls ; everything produces a singular effect upon him. Again, all at once he is thrown, quite unprepared, upon a new and trying experience ; for now he meets the groaning ambulance and the bloody stretcher. He meets limping, armless, legless, disfigured, wounded men. To the right of him and to the left of him are the lifeless forms of the slain. Suddenly a large iron missile of death strikes close beside him and explodes, sending out twenty or more jagged fragments, which remorselessly maim or kill five or six of his mates before they have had the opportunity to strike one blow for their country. His face is now very pale ; and will not the American soldier flinch and turn back? There is a stone wall! there is a building! there is a stack of hay! it is so easy to hide! But no. He will not be a coward. "O God, support and strengthen me!" 'Tis all his prayer. Soon he is at work. Yonder is the foe! "Load and fire!" "Load and fire!" But the cry comes, "Our flank is turned!" "Our men retreat!" With tears pouring down his cheek, he slowly yields, and joins the retiring throng. Without any more nerve and little strength, he struggles back from a lost field. Now he drinks the dregs of suffering. Without blanket for the night, without food, without hope, it is no wonder that a panic seizes him and he runs demoralized away.

This disreputable course, however, is only temporary. The soldier before long forgets his defeats and his sufferings, brightens up his armor, and resumes his place on the defensive line. He submits for weary days to discipline, drill, and hard fare; he wades through the snows of winter and the deep mud of a Virginia spring. He sleeps upon the ground, upon the deck of transport steamer, and upon the floor of the platform car. He helps load and unload stores; he makes fascines and gabions ; he corduroys quicksands, and bridges creeks and bogs. Night and day he digs, or watches in the trenches.

What a world of new experience! What peculiar labor and suffering he passes through, the soldier alone can tell you. He now marches hurriedly to his second battle ; soon after he is in a series of them. Fight and fall back! Fight and fall back! Oh those days of hopelessness, sorrow, toil, and emaciation! How vividly the living soldier remembers them, those days when he cried from the bottom of his heart. " O God, how long! how long!" Would you have patience to follow him through the commingling of disasters from the battle of Cedar Mountain to the same old Bull Run, you would emerge with him from the chaos and behold his glistening bayonet again on the successful field of Antietam, where a glimmer of hope lighted up his heart. Would you go with him to the bloody fields of Fredericksburg, staunch his wounds in the wilderness of Chancellorsville, and journey on with him afterwards to this hallowed ground of Gettysburg; and could you be enabled to read and record his toils, his sufferings, and all his thoughts, you might be able to appreciate the true American soldier. You might then recite the first chapter of the cost of the preservation of the American Union.

In September, 1863, after the battle of Gettysburg, the Government sends two army corps to reinforce our brethren in the West. The soldier is already far from home and friends, but he is suddenly apprised that he must go two thousand miles further. He cannot visit his family to take leave of them. He has scarcely the opportunity of writing a line of farewell. The chances of death are multitudinous as they appear before his imagination, and the hope of returning is very slender. Yet again the soldier does not falter. With forty others he crowds into the close, unventilated freight car, and speeds away, night and day, without even the luxury of a decent seat. With all the peculiar discomforts of this journey, the backings and the waitings at the railroad junctions, the transfers from car to car, and from train to train ; being confined for days without the solace and strength derived from his coffee, there is yet something compensative in the exhilerating influence of change. And there is added to it, in passing through Ohio and Indiana, a renewed inspiration as the people turn out in masses to welcome him and to bid him God speed; as little girls throw wreaths of flowers round his neck, kiss his bronzed cheek, and strew his car with other offerings of love and devotion. Such impressions as were here received were never effaced. They touched the rough heart anew with tenderness, and, being a reminder of all the old home affections, only served to deepen his resolution sooner or later, by the blessing of God, to reach the goal of his ambition; that is to say, with his compatriots, to secure to his children, and to other children, *enduring peace*, with liberty and an undivided country. He passes on through Kentucky, through the battle fields of Tennessee, already historical. The names. Nashville, Stone River, Murfreesboro, and Tullahoma, remind him of past struggles and portend future conflicts. He is deposited at Bridgeport, Alabama, a houseless, cheerless, chilly place, on the banks of the Tennessee; possessing no interest further than that furnished by the railroad bridge destroyed, and the yet remaining rubbish and filth of an enemy's camp.

Before many days the soldier threads his way up the valley of the great river which winds and twists amid the rugged mountains, till he finds himself beneath the rock-crowned steeps of Lookout. Flash after flash, volume after volume of light-colored smoke, and peal on peal of cannon, the crashing sound of shot and the screaming of shell, are the ominous signs of unfriendly welcome sent forth to meet him from this rocky height. Yet on he marches, in spite of threatening danger, in spite of the ambush along his route, until he has joined hands with his Western brother, who had come from Chattanooga to meet and to greet him.

This is where the valley of Lookout joins that of the Tennessee. At this place the stories of Eastern and Western hardship, suffering, battling, and danger, are recapitulated and made to blend into the common history and the common sacrifice of the American soldier.

Were there time I would gladly take you step by step with the soldier as he bridges and crosses the broad and rapid river; as he ascends and storms the height of Mission Ridge; or as he plants his victorious feet, waves his banner, and flashes his gun on the top of Lookout Mountain. I would carry you with him across the death-bearing streams of Chickamauga. I would have you follow him in his weary, barefooted, wintry march to the relief of Knoxville and back to Chattanooga. From this point of view I would open up the spring campaign, where the great General initiated his remarkable work of genius and daring. I could point you to the soldier pursuing the enemy into the strongholds of Dalton, behind the stern, impassable features of Rocky Face.

Resaca, Adairsville, Cassville, Dallas, New Hope Church, Pickett's Mill, Pine Top, Lost Mountain, Kenesaw, Culp's Farm, Smyrna, Camp Ground, Peach Tree Creek, Atlanta, from so many points of view, and Jonesboro, are names of battle fields upon each of which a soldier's memory dwells. For upwards of a hundred days he scarcely rested from the conflict. He skirmished over rocks, hills and mountains; through mud, streams and forests. For hundreds of miles he gave his aid to dig that endless chain of entrenchments which compassed every one of the enemy's fortified positions. He companied with those who combatted the obstinate foe on the front and on the flanks of those mountain fastnesses which the enemy had deemed impregnable, and he had a right at last to echo the sentiment of his indefatigable leader, " Atlanta is ours, and fairly won." Could you now have patience to turn back with him and fight these battles over again, behold his communications cut, his railroad destroyed for miles and miles; enter the bloody fight of Alatoona, follow him through the forced marches, *via* Rome, in Georgia, away back to Resaca, and through the obstructed gaps of the mountains into Alabama, you would thank God for giving him a stout heart and an unflinching faith in a just and noble cause. Weary and worn, he reposed at Atlanta, on his return, but one single night, when he commenced the memorable march toward Savannah.

The soldier has become a veteran; he can march all day with his musket, his knapsack, his cartridge-box, his haversack and canteen upon his person; his muscles have become large and rigid, so that what was once extremely difficult he now accomplishes with graceful ease. This fact must be borne in mind when studying the soldiers' marches through Georgia and the Carolinas.

The enemy burned every bridge across stream after stream; the rivers, bordered with swamps—for example, the Ocmulgee, the Oconee, and the Ogechee—were defended at every crossing. That they were passed at all by our forces, is due to the cheerful, fearless, indomitable private soldier. Oh that you had seen him, as I have, wading creeks a half mile in width, and water waist deep, under fire, pressing on through wide swamps, without one faltering step, charging in line upon the most formidable works, which were well defended! You could then appreciate him and what he has accomplished as I do. You could then feel the poignant sorrow that I always felt when I saw him fall bleeding to the earth.

I must now leave the soldier to tell his own tale amongst the people, of his bold, bloody work at McAllister, against the torpedoes, abattis, artillery, and musketry; of his privations at Savannah; of his struggles through the swamps, quicksands, and over the broad rivers of the Carolinas; of the fights, fires, explosions, doubts, and triumphs suggested by Griswoldville, Rivers' and Binnaker's bridges, Orangeburg, Congaree creek, Columbia, Cheraw, Fayetteville, Averysboro, and Bentonville. I will leave him to tell how his hopes brightened at the reunion at Goldsboro; how his heart throbbed with gratitude and joy as the wires confirmed the rumored news of Lee's defeat, so soon to be followed by the capture of the enemy's Capitol and of his entire army. I will leave him to tell to yourselves and your children, how he felt and acted, how proud was his bearing, how elastic his step, as he marched in review before the President of the United States at Washington. I would do the soldier injustice not to say that there was one thing wanting to make his satisfaction complete, and that was the sight of the tall form of Abraham Lincoln, and the absence of that bitter recollection which he could not altogether exclude from his heart—that *he* had died by the hand of a traitor assassin.

I have given you only glimpses of the American soldier, as I have seen him. To feel the full force of what he has done and suffered, you should have accompanied him for the last four years. You should have stood upon the battle fields during and after the struggle; and you should have completed your observation in the army hospitals, and upon the countless grounds peopled with the dead. The maimed bodies, the multitude of graves, the historic fields, the monumental stones like this we are laying to-day, after all are only meagre memorials of the soldiers' work. God grant that what he planted, nourished, and has now preserved by his blood—I mean *American liberty*—may be a plant dear to us as the apple of the eye, and that its growth may not be hindered till its roots are firmly set in every State of this Union, and till the full fruition of its blessed fruit is realized by men of every name, color and description, in this broad land.

Now, as I raise my eyes and behold the place where my friend and trusted commander, General Reynolds, fell, let me add my own testimonial to that of others, that we lost in him a true patriot, a true man, a complete General, and a thorough soldier. Upon him, and the others who died here for their country, let there never cease to descend the most earnest benediction of every American heart.

Let me congratulate this noble Keystone State that it was able to furnish such tried and able men as Reynolds who fell, and Meade who lived to guide us successfully through this wonderful and hotly contested battle.

In the midst of all conflicts, of all sorrows and triumphs, let us never for an instant forget that there is a God in heaven whose arm is strong to help, whose balm is sweet to assuage every pain, and whose love embraces all joy. To Him, then, let us look in gratitude and praise that it has been His will so greatly to bless our nation; and may this Monument ever remind us and our posterity, in view of the fact that we prevailed against our enemies, "that righteousness exalteth a nation, but sin is a reproach to any people."

POEM.

BY CHARLES G. HALPINE,
("Miles O'Reilly.")

As men beneath some pang of grief
  Or sudden joy will dumbly stand,
Finding no words to give relief—
Clear, passion-warm, complete and brief—
  To thoughts with which their souls expand;
So here to-day—these trophies nigh—
  Our trembling lips no utterance reach;
The hills around, the graves, the sky—
The silent poem of the eye
  Surpasses all the art of speech!

To-day, a Nation meets to build
  A Nation's trophy to the dead
Who, living, formed the sword and shield—
The arms she sadly learned to wield
  When other hope of peace had fled.
And not alone for those who lie
  In honored graves before us blent,
Shall our proud column, broad and high,
Climb upward to the blessing sky,
  But be for all a monument.

An emblem of our grief, as well
  For others as for these, we raise;
For these beneath our feet who dwell,
And all who in the Good Cause fell
  On other fields, in other frays.

To all the self-same love we bear,
    Which here for marbled memory strives;
No soldier for a wreath would care
Which all true comrades might not share—
    Brothers in death as in their lives!

On Southern hill-sides, parched and brown,
    In tangled swamp, on verdant ridge,
Where pines and broadening oaks look down,
And jasmine weaves its yellow crown,
    And trumpet-creepers clothe the hedge;
Along the shores of endless sand,
    Beneath the palms of Southern plains,
Sleep everywhere, hand locked in hand,
The brothers of the gallant band
    Who here poured life through throbbing veins.

Around the closing eyes of all
    The same red glories glared and flew—
The hurrying flags, the bugle call,
The whistle of the angry ball,
    The elbow-touch of comrades true;
The skirmish fire—a spattering spray;
    The long, sharp growl of fire by file,
The thickening fury of the fray
When opening batteries get in play,
    And the lines form o'er many a mile.

The foeman's yell, our answering cheer,
    Red flashes through the gathering smoke,
Swift orders, resonant and clear,
Blithe cries from comrades tried and dear,
    The shell-scream and the sabre-stroke;
The rolling fire from left to right,
    From right to left, we hear it swell;
The headlong charges swift and bright,
The thickening tumult of the fight
    And bursting thunders of the shell.

Now deadlier, denser grows the strife,
  And here we yield and there we gain;
The air with hurtling missiles rife,
Volley for volley, life for life—
  No time to heed the cries of pain!
Panting as up the hills we charge,
  Or down them as we broken roll;
Life never felt so high, so large;
And never o'er so wide a marge,
  In triumph swept the kindling soul!

New raptures waken in the breast
  Amid this hell of scene and sound;
The barking batteries never rest,
And broken foot, by horsemen pressed,
  Still stubbornly contest their ground.
Fresh waves of battle rolling in
  To take the place of shattered waves;
Torn lines that grow more bent and thin—
A blinding crowd, a maddening din—
  'Twas thus were filled these very graves!

Night falls at length with pitying veil—
  A moonlit silence deep and fresh;
These upturned faces, stained and pale,
Vainly the chill night dews assail—
  Far colder than the dews their flesh!
And flickering far through brush and wood
  Go searching parties, torch in hand—
"Seize if you can some rest and food,
At dawn the fight will be renewed;
  Sleep on your arms!" the hushed command.

They talk in whispers as they lie
  In line—these rough and weary men;
"Dead or but wounded?" then a sigh;
"No coffee either!" "Guess we'll try
  To get those two guns back again."

"We five flags to their one! oho!"
"That bridge—'twas hot there as we passed!"
"The colonel dead! It can't be so;
Wounded and badly—that I know;
But he kept saddle to the last."

"Be sure to send it if I fall—"
"Any tobacco? Bill, have you?"
"A brown-haired, blue-eyed, laughing doll—"
"Good-night, boys, and God keep you all!"
"What! sound asleep? Guess I'll sleep too."
"Yes, just about this hour they pray
For Dad." "Stop talking! pass the word!"
And soon as quiet as the clay,
Which thousands will but be next day,
The long-drawn sighs of sleep are heard.

Oh, men! to whom this sketch, though rude,
Calls back some scene of pain and pride;
Oh, widow! hugging close your brood;
Oh, wife! with happiness renewed,
Since he again is at your side;
This trophy that to-day we raise,
Should be a monument for all;
And on its sides no niggard phrase
Confine a generous Nation's praise
To those who here have chanced to fall.

But let us all to-day combine
Still other monuments to raise;
Here for the dead we build a shrine;
And now to those who, crippled, pine,
Let us give hope of happier days:—
Let homes for these sad wrecks of war,
Through all the land with speed arise;
Tongues cry from every gaping scar,
Let not our brother's tomb debar
The wounded living from your eyes."

A noble day, a deed as good:
  A noble scene in which 'tis done;
The Birthday of our Nationhood:
And here again the Nation stood
  On this same day—its life rewon!
A bloom of banners in the air,
  A double calm of sky and soul;
Triumphal chant and bugle blare,
And green fields, spreading bright and fair,
  While heavenward our hosannas roll.

Hosannas for a land redeemed,
  The bayonet sheathed, the cannon dumb;
Passed, as some horror we have dreamed,
The fiery meteors that here streamed,
  Threatening within our homes to come!
Again our banner floats abroad,
  Gone the one stain that on it fell—
And, bettered by His chastening rod,
With streaming eyes uplift to God,
  We say, "HE DOETH ALL THINGS WELL."

HYMN

TO THE MEMORY OF OUR FALLEN HEROES AT THE BATTLE OF GETTYSBURG, PENNSYLVANIA.

(Sung by the National Union Musical Association of Baltimore.)

Hark! a nation's sigh ascend;
Hark! a thousand voices blend;
From your thrones of glory bend,
  Sons of liberty.

From each dark empurpled field,
Where your blood the Union sealed,
Spirit-tongues to-day have pealed
  The soldier's requiem.

Where the smoke of battle curled,
Where the bolt of death was hurled,
Ye our starry flag unfurl'd,
  Floating o'er the free.

In the dark and trying hour,
Putting forth your steady power,
Caused the Rebel hordes to cower,
  Just two years ago.

Flashing sword and burning word,
Southrons felt and Southrons heard—
Plumed our country's banner-bird,
  Just two years ago.

Martyred sons of trying days,
While the world resounds your praise,
Hear the songs your children raise,
  Sons of liberty.

REMARKS OF HIS EXCELLENCY A. G. CURTIN,

GOVERNOR OF PENNSYLVANIA.

THE programme for the exercises of the occasion having been fulfilled, calls were made by all the people present for Governor Curtin, who spoke in substance as follows:

Having learned last week that my name occurred on the programme for the ceremonies of this occasion, I immediately asked that it should be omitted. There did not seem to be time for such preparation as would be proper for a ceremonial like this. I am deeply grateful for your hearty and enthusiastic request that I should be heard, and I will draw upon the inspirations of the time and the place, the connection between the event and this Sabbath day of American Freedom, and the hallowed precincts within which we all stand.

It would seem to be proper for me to express the thanks of the people of Pennsylvania to the citizens of the United States, who join with us to-day, and who have hitherto contributed their influence and means to the erection of this place of sepulture for the remains of those who perished in the great battles of Gettysburg, and who this day surround the foundation-stone of a monument to their memory. We thank the citizens of the eighteen States who have given valuable and voluntary service, as trustees of the association, representing their respective States. We thank the people who have come up here in multitudes to participate in these solemnities. We thank that patriotic and benevolent brotherhood, so well represented here to-day by its chiefs, for their ancient rites and ceremonies, for their words of fraternity and love, contributed and pronounced upon the corner-stone of this structure, which is to be the Monument of the devotion and fidelity to country of their brothers and ours. And we are fortunate in having here with us, my fellow-citizens, the great chief who commanded the historic Army of the Potomac, on the signal day which made his fame and that of his Army, forever illustrious in the annals of American history; and we express with one voice our thanks to him and his brave companions, so many of whom remain to surround him here, and honor us with their presence. But more than all, my fellow-citizens, let us all unite in our expressions of gratitude to the sublime heroism and unselfish patriotism of the private soldiers of the Republic; for to them, above all others, we owe the safety of our free Government, and the return of the blessings of peace and tranquility to our distressed country. I could not but feel the unselfishness of the words of the chosen orator of the day; and the armless sleeve of the maimed General, seemed of itself eloquent, when he forgot the statesmen and generals of the war, and gave credit to the private soldier for all the glories which now surround the blood-stained, but forever stable, institutions of American liberty.

Our Monument should be the choicest work of art on this continent; it should be made beautiful and strong. This place will forever be attractive; the statesman can here meditate on the sacrifices made for liberty and civilization; the soldier can study the faultless plan of battle; and all can count here, the cost to this generation of maintaining the principles of freedom, transmitted to us from our ancestors. But no work of art can express our feelings of gratitude for the soldier of the Republic, living or dead; he has his memory enshrined in the hearts of a grateful people,—" there a monument that needs no scroll."

But why should I speak to you to-day? It is but two years since the death-struggle of rebellion and treason filled this valley, now so peaceful, with bloodshed and carnage; and the thunders of the artillery of that eventful strife will speak to man for his freedom and individuality, until time shall be no more.

Stronger than logic, sweeter than poetry, the orators of this occasion lie in their graves around you; no living lips can reach your hearts as does the mute eloquence which comes up from the graves of the heroic dead. We are all of one family, my fellow-citizens, the living and the dead; those who lie around us shed benefactions upon us by the good they did; let us this day draw inspiration from their sublime virtues, and strive like them to be faithful to the Government they died to save.

We people of Pennsylvania give praise to God that it was of His mysterious providence that the blood of the people of eighteen States, here represented, should seal a covenant, made in the hour of the nation's deepest agony, that this great republic shall be for ever sacred to Union and fraternity, and pray Him that the lessons of Gettysburg shall sink deeply into the American heart.

The remarks of Governor Curtin were uttered with a fervor and earnestness that fastened the attention of the whole audience, and from their impassioned effect, the reporters failed to take them down as fully as delivered.

The Benediction was pronounced by the Rev. D. T. Carnahan.

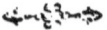

EXERCISES

AT THE

DEDICATION OF THE MONUMENT

IN THE

Soldiers' National Cemetery at Gettysburg.

JULY 1st, 1869.

The Dedicatory Prayer was made by the Rev. Henry Ward Beecher

The Dedication of the Monument.

ADDRESS OF MAJOR-GENERAL GEORGE G. MEADE.

MY Fellow-Citizens, Ladies and Gentlemen.—Six years ago I stood upon this ground under circumstances very different from those which now surround us. These beautiful hills and valleys, teeming with luxuriant crops, these happy faces around me, are widely different from the tumultuous roar of war and the terrible scenes enacted at that time. Four years ago I stood here, by invitation of some honorable gentlemen who have brought me here this time, and laid the corner-stone of the Monument which we are brought here to-day to dedicate; and now, for the third time, I appear before you at the request of the managers of the Monument Association, to render my assistance, humble as it is, in paying respect to the memory of the brave men who fell here, by dedicating this Monument to them; and at the request of these gentlemen I am about to make to you a few, a very few remarks which are incident to this occasion and suggested by it. When I look around and see, as I now see, so many brave men who were by my side in that memorable battle, among them his Excellency the present Governor of Pennsylvania, General Geary, and others who were with me at that time; when I look back and think upon the noble spirits who then fought so well, and now sleep that sleep that knows no waking—gallant Reynolds, my bosom friend, as well as my right hand officer; brave Vincent, and Zook, and Weed, and others, far more in number than I have time of words to mention,—my feelings are those of mingled sadness and joy,—sadness, my friends, to think that there ever was an occasion when such men should be arrayed in battle, as they were here; that we should ever have been called upon, as we were upon this field, to defend the flag of our country and Government, which had been handed down to us from our forefathers. It is sad to think of the mourning and desolation which prostrated our whole land, North and South; it is sad to contemplate the vast destruction of life which we here wrought in obedience to our highest duty. I am filled with sadness to think of the host of mourning widows and orphans left throughout the land by that deadly struggle. Such thoughts necessarily crowd upon us. At the same time I give thanks to the Almighty, who directed the event, and who selected me as an humble instrument, with those then around me upon this field, to obtain that decisive victory which turned the tide of that great war, and settled for ever the trust in this country of the great principles of personal liberty and constitutional freedom. I feel grateful, too, that our fellow-countrymen have been moved to such respect and honor as we are now paying to the memory of those men who, in the discharge of their duty, laid down their lives, proving, by the highest sacrifice man can render, their devotion to the cause they were defending. Gratitude to those present to-day, who, by their presence, contribute to render the high honor justly due to the fallen brave.

There is one subject, my friends, which I will mention now and on this spot, while my attention is being called to it, and on which I trust my feeble voice will have some influence. When I contemplate this field, I see here and there the marks of hastily dug trenches in which repose the dead against whom we fought. They are the work of my brothers in arms the day after the battle. Above them a bit of plank indicates simply that these remains of the fallen were hurriedly laid there by soldiers who met them in battle. Why should we not collect them in some suitable place? I do not ask that a monument be erected over them; I do not ask that we should in any way endorse their cause or their conduct, or entertain other than feelings of condemnation for their course; but they are dead! They have gone before their Maker to be judged. In all civilized countries it is the usage to bury the dead with decency and respect, and even to fallen enemies respectful burial is accorded in death. I earnestly hope that this suggestion may have some influence throughout our broad land, for this is only one of a hundred crowded battle fields. Some persons may be designated by the Government to collect these neglected bones and bury them without commemorating monuments, simply indicating that below sleep misguided men who fell in battle for a cause over which we triumphed.

I shall delay you no longer, for you are about to listen to one of the most eloquent men in this country. My purpose was simply to comply with the kind invitation given me to speak meet words of praise for the dead heroes sleeping around, and to aid in the solemnities of this occasion. I thank you for your attention, and will now unveil the statue.

THE DEDICATION OF THE MONUMENT IN THE

ORATION OF GOVERNOR O. P. MORTON.

When the Monument we are about to dedicate shall have crumbled into dust; when the last vestige of this Cemetery shall have been obliterated by the hand of time; when there shall be nothing left of all that we see now but the hills, the valleys, the streams and the distant mountains, the great battle which here took place, with its far-reaching consequences, will still live in history. Nations have their birth, youth, maturity, old age and death; and ours, though we call it eternal, and our institutions immortal, will be no exception. But though nations must pass away, and all physical evidence of their existence be lost, yet may they live through all time in the brightness of their examples, in the glory of their deeds, and in the beneficence of their institutions. These are the inheritances they leave to the far-coming centuries.

When the pyramids of Egypt shall have sunk to the level of the Nile; when the last remnant of Grecian architecture, the last inscribed block of marble shall have perished, men will still read of Moses and the Pass of Thermopylæ. Monuments, after all, are but for the present, and may only instruct a few generations. But a glorious deed is a joy forever.

Six years ago, day after to-morrow, the Union army was stretched along these heights from Culp's Hill to Round Top—a human breakwater, against which the great tidal wave of rebellion was to dash in vain, and be thrown back in bloody spray and broken billows. The Rebel chieftain, flushed by his successes at Fredericksburg and Chancellorsville, forgetting that his triumphs had arisen from the fact that he had fought upon his own soil, behind natural fastnesses, having the advantage of choice of position and knowledge of the country, had insolently crossed the Potomac and invaded the loyal State of Pennsylvania. But from this invasion he was hurled back in bloody defeat, and in disordered flight crossed the Potomac, never again to set foot upon the soil of a loyal State. On yonder high ground across the plain was drawn out in battle array the Rebel host. It was an open field; the terms were nearly equal; and steady Northern valor, animated by the love of country, was to meet the boasted chivalry of the South fighting for slavery, sweep it from the field, strip it of its meretricious plumes, and give the Confederacy a fatal wound.

It is the solid qualities of men and nations that win in the long run. The chivalry of false pride, the arrogance and vanity of a favored class, whose elevation is only seen by the depression of others, may, by spasmodic efforts for a time dazzle the eyes of the world, but cannot long maintain a successful contest with truth, justice, and the strength of free institutions. This was illustrated in the war of the Rebellion, and in the battle of Gettysburg. This battle was not won by superior strategy or military genius, although managed with great courage and skill by General Meade and his subordinate commanders, who left nothing undone that the occasion seemed to require, and who made the best use of the forces and opportunities at their command.

It was a three days' battle, with varying fortunes the first and second days, in which the steadiness of Northern valor, animated by the convictions of a just cause, and the love and pride of a great and free country, finally wore out, bore down, and swept from the field the Rebel masses, composed of men of equal physical courage, but whose moral powers were impaired by the absence of that strong conviction of the right which is a vast element of success.

In yonder Cemetery, among the white tombstones, " where heaves the turf in many a mouldering heap " over the buried generations of the hamlet, was planted the artillery whose fearful peals would have aroused the slumbering dead were it not ordained that they should awake only at the sound of the last trump. Just behind the crest of the hill, in the old cemetery, stood the tent of our glorious commander, the imperturbable Meade, calmly dictating his orders, while the storm of shot and shell flew over and around him. From yonder steeple, southwest of the village, the Rebel chieftain surveyed the field, directed his host, and from time to time saw his advancing columns reel and wither, and finally retreat in hopeless flight and confusion. The flower of the Rebel army had been chosen for the assault, and were massed to bring overwhelming numbers to bear on the point of attack. The Rebel chieftain brought together more than one hundred and fifty pieces of artillery, with which, for three hours, he poured a terrific fire upon that part of the Union lines he intended to assault.

It was a grand and solemn sight, when line after line, with steady step and in perfect order, emerged from the smoke and swept across the field towards the Union army. It was a moment of vast peril and import, of which both parties were powerfully conscious. If the Rebel assault was successful and we lost the battle, Washington and Philadelphia were within their grasp. The North invaded, defeated, and demoralized would do—we know not what. Foreign nations would be encouraged to intervene, and the South, elated, would put forth more desperate efforts than before. If the assault failed and we gained the battle, the remnant of the Rebel hosts must seek safety in flight, and a blow would be inflicted upon the Confederacy from which it could scarcely recover. These thoughts were present in the minds of all, and gave heroic courage to assault and to resist. But now the fire of our artillery is opened upon the advancing columns, and the shot and shell tore through their ranks, making great gaps, which were quickly filled up by those who came behind. But onward they came with desperate courage, until soon the fierce fire of musketry on both sides mingled with the horrid roar of artillery. Then, with terrific yells, they rushed upon our lines; but the impetus of their assault was suddenly checked. They were met with a courage as desperate as their own, and a fierce hand-to-hand conflict took place. The result was not long doubtful. Their thinned and broken columns were flung back across the plain in headlong flight, leaving thousands of prisoners in our hands, the ground covered with dead and dying, and wet and muddy with blood. We had gained the day, though at fearful cost. The victory was great and mighty in its consequences. The prestige of the Rebel army was broken, never to be recovered, and the wound inflicted upon the Confederacy was never staunched until it had bled to death.

The next day was the Fourth of July, and the most memorable since that of 1776. On another field it witnessed the surrender of another large Rebel army to the great chieftain of the war, now our illustrious President. The capture of Vicksburg opened the navigation of the Mississippi river, and severed from the Confederacy all that part of its territory lying west of that river. The loss to the Confederacy was irreparable. It was cut off from its chief source of supplies. The limits of the war were greatly circumscribed. The mass of the Rebel population was demoralized and began to despair. From that day it became manifest that the Rebellion could not succeed, unless the Southern people exhibited that endurance, patience under adversity, and high devotion that will sacrifice everything for the cause, which, as it turned out, they did not possess. By our victories at Gettysburg and Vicksburg the Rebellion lost its prestige in Europe, and all hopes of foreign intervention.

At the foot of the Monument sleep the heroes of the battle. Here lies the father, the husband, the brother and the only son. In far off homes, among the hills of New England, on the shores of the lakes, and in the valleys and plains of the West, the widow, the orphan, and the aged parents are weeping for these beloved dead. Many of the tombs are marked " unknown," but they will all be recognized on the morning of the resurrection. The unknown dead left behind them kindred, friends, and breaking hearts. None die so humble but leave some one to mourn. " Perished at Gettysburg, in defence of their country," nine hundred and seventy-nine men of whose names, homes, or lineage there is no trace left on earth. Doubtless the recording angel has preserved the record, and when the books are opened on the last day their names will be found in letters of light on the immortal page of heroes who died that their country might live.

In the fields before us are the graves of the Rebel dead, now sunk to the level of the plain, " unmarked, unhonored and unknown." They were our countrymen— of our blood, language, and history. They displayed a courage worthy of their country, and of a better cause, and we may drop a tear to their memory. The news of this fatal field carried agony to thousands of Southern homes, and the wail of despair was heard in the everglades and orange groves of the South. Would to God that these men had died for their country and not in fratricidal strife, for its destruction. Oh, who can describe the wickedness of rebellion, or paint the horrors of civil war!

The Rebellion was madness. It was the insanity of States, the delirium of millions, brought on by the pernicious influence of human slavery. The people of the South were drunk with the spoils of the labor of four millions of slaves. They were educated in the belief that chivalry and glory were the inheritance only of slaveholders; that free institutions and free labor begat cowardice and servility; that Northern men were sordid and mercenary, intent only upon gain, and would not fight for their Government or principles. And thus educated, and thus believing, they raised their hands to strike the Government of their fathers and to establish a new constitution, the chief corner-stone of which was to be human slavery.

The lust of power, the unholy greed of slavery, the mad ambition of disappointed statesmen impelled the people of the South to a fearful crime, which drenched the land with fraternal blood, that has been punished as few crimes have ever been in this world, but out of which, we are assured, that God in His providence will bring forth the choicest blessings to our country and to the human race; even as of the dead. Liberty universal, soon to be guaranteed and preserved by suffrage universal; the keeping of a nation's freedom to be entrusted to *all the people*, and not to a part only; the national reproach washed out in rivers of blood, it is true; but the sins of the world were atoned by the blood of the Saviour, and the expiation of blood seems to be the grand economy of God founded in wisdom, to mortals inscrutable. Resurrection comes only from the grave. Death is the great progenitor of life. From the tomb of the Rebellion a nation has been born again. The principles of liberty, so gloriously stated in the Declaration of Independence, had hitherto existed in theory. The Government had ever been a painful contradiction to the Declaration. While proclaiming to the world that liberty was the gift of God to every human being, four millions of the people were held in abject and brutalizing slavery, under the shadow of the national flag. In the presence of these slaves, professions of devotion to liberty were vain and hypocritical. The clanking of their chains ascended perpetually in contradiction to our professions, and the enemies of republicanism pointed contemptuously to our example. But all this is passed. Slavery lies buried in the tomb of the Rebellion. The Rebellion, the offspring of slavery, hath murdered its unnatural parent, and the perfect reign of liberty is at hand.

With the ratification of the fifteenth article, proposed by Congress as an amendment to the Constitution of the United States, which we have every reason to believe will soon be completed, impartial suffrage will be established throughout the land. The equal rights of men will be recognized, and the millennium in liberty and government will be realized, to which our fathers looked forward with hopefulness and joy.

The principles of liberty once planted in the earth, and ripened into their rich fruits, will be borne through all the ages, blessing mankind to the latest generation, even as the seeds first sown by the hand of God in paradise, were blown by the winds from continent to continent, until the world was clothed with verdure, fruits and flowers.

The prospect for liberty throughout the world was never so bright as it is to-day. In all civilized lands the grand armies of freedom are on their march. And they are allied armies. Victory to one will give prestige and confidence to the others. With some, progress will be slow; they will encounter disaster and defeat, but will again rally, and go forward to final victory. In the great campaign of freedom we count, not by months, but by decades and generations, in which there will be many a Bull Run, many a Gettysburg, and a final Appomattox. The lines of march will be marked by many a cemetery like this, by the wrecks of fallen institutions and dynasties, and by the ruins of hereditary privilege and caste.

Let us briefly review the advance of liberty since 1776.

The principles of the Declaration of Independence took early and deep root in France. The people of the empire had long suffered from the grossest misrule and oppression, and their minds were well prepared to comprehend and accept the new gospel of Liberty. The French revolution first threw off the kingly government, then established complete democracy, but not knowing how to use liberty without abusing it, the people being governed by their passions, and seeking to avenge upon parties and classes the wrongs they had suffered for generations, passed into anarchy, from which the transition back to monarchy and despotism was easy and rapid. But the return of monarchy was not characterized by the former oppression and misrule. The people had learned their rights and monarchs had learned their power. Many of the old abuses which had been swept away by the revolution were gone forever, and the new monarchy governed with comparative justice, liberality, and humanity.

The spirit of liberty had entered into the hearts of the people, and from time to time asserted itself in various ways, and in 1848 France returned again to a republic. This lasted but a short time, but the new monarch who overthrew it and established himself upon its ruins was constrained to acknowledge the sovereignty of the people, and to profess to accept his crown by the vote of the majority. While we cannot say much for the freedom of that election, nor believe that the result was the will of the people, yet it was of vast significance that the usurping government was compelled to claim its title from a pretended popular election. In many respects the government of Napoleon III. has been excellent. He has recognized the freedom of religious opinion. He has protected the people in their persons and property. He has encouraged trade and industry, stimulated manufactures, and extended their commerce. He has given them a constitution which creates a legislative body, and guarantees many rights and privileges. But the people are not satisfied. They are denied liberty of speech and of the press on political questions. They are not allowed to assemble for the discussion of measures in which they are vitally interested. Their legislative body is so constructed and managed as to be a mere registry of the will of the Emperor. The recent elections show the spirit of discontent and the existence of a powerful party who understand their rights and are determined to assert them, peacefully, if they can, and, as we have reason to believe, forcibly, if they must. The attentive observer and student of French history, is led to the conclusion that nothing can preserve the throne and dynasty of Napoleon III., but the concession of the popular rights and the establishment of freedom of speech and of the press, of the elections, and of the legislative body. The republican sentiment of France, though it has been unfortunate, and from time to time suppressed and apparently extinguished, is still vital, is growing in intelligence and power, and cannot be restrained, unless monarchy becomes so liberal and free as to confer the substantial benefit of a republic. We cannot doubt that Napoleon appreciates the situation, and is preparing to make such concessions as will keep the popular discontent this side of revolution.

The march of liberty in Germany is slow but steady. The great German family are struggling for unity and freedom. The institutions of Germany are becoming more liberal from year to year, and the condition of the people better and happier. The evil of large standing armies, annually withdrawing the young men from home and productive pursuits, is still endured, because Germany is surrounded by warlike and powerful enemies, clad in complete armor. But everywhere the tendency of the German mind is to the fullest liberty of thought, and to the recognition of the " equal rights " of men.

Austria, so long oppressed, reels and responds to the impulse of liberty. An intelligent Emperor, who has not shut his eyes to what is going on in the world around him, perceives that he cannot stem the powerful current everywhere setting in toward free institutions, and that the security of his throne depends upon his conceding to the people rights and privileges which have been denied them since Austria was an empire, and giving back to Hungary the enjoyment of her ancient constitution. The abolition of the Concordat, the establishment of religious freedom, the equal taxation of all classes, are among the hopeful beginnings of Austrian reform.

Italy, the ancient seat of the power and glory of the Roman Empire, land of history, philosophy, poetry, music, painting, sculpture, and romance, land of " starry climes and sunny skies," whose delicious climate, lofty mountains, and beautiful valleys and plains have ever excited the admiration of the traveller and poet, has made great progress in unity and freedom. Suffrage nearly universal, the habeas corpus, freedom of religion and free schools are some of the principal features of Italian liberty.

The spirit of liberty is abroad in Russia—mighty empire of the North, whose government has represented the perfect idea of absolute despotism—an autocrat power, unrestrained by constitution or law. An enlightened Czar, animated by love for his people, and perceiving the individual happiness and material prosperity produced by free institutions, abolished slavery throughout his dominions, made the serfs freemen, and gave to them local free institutions, based upon the right of suffrage. It is true the imperial power still extends over all—a dark, impenetrable canopy—but beneath its shadow there is individual liberty and local self-government. Thus far the prosperous result has established the wisdom of the Czar, and may we not believe that he has laid the foundation of a free government, to be developed into a grand republic in the far future?—and nearer, into a constitutional monarchy, with representative institutions? Liberty is like living seed; wherever planted it vivifies, expands, develops. Thus planted in Russia among the lowest people, and for local purposes, it will grow, develop, and finally conquer. Russia is among the progressive nations, and is our friend, and it was the American example which touched the heart and intellect of the Emperor.

The spirit of liberty in its onward march has invaded Spain, and is stirring the great national heart. We have lately seen the great Spanish people firmly, and almost peacefully and unanimously, depose a licentious queen and declare against her dynasty. We have seen this people meet in primary assemblies, and, by suffrage universal, elect a National Cortes which has for many months, in calm debate, considered and framed a new constitution, which, although not republican in its form, contains so much liberty, so much that is good and progressive in government, as to give the world high hope in the future of Spain. We have heard this national assembly declare that all sovereignty and power reside in the people, thus denying the divine rights of kings, and asserting the fundamental idea of free institutions. We have heard it pronounce the abolition of slavery. We have heard it pronounce the right of all men to worship God according to the dictates of their own consciences. Verily, these are great things and new times in old Spain. These are the germs of free institutions, and will, in the progress of years, grow into a republican government.

Cuba, the queen of the Antilles, richest gem in the Spanish crown, the most fertile of islands, rich beyond description in the fruits and productions of tropical climes, and from which the Spanish treasury has so long been supplied, is making a bold, vigorous, and, as we trust, a successful effort to throw off the Spanish yoke and establish her independence. The native Cubans, inspired by the spirit of liberty, have proclaimed liberty to the slaves, freedom of religious opinion, and that governments exist only by the consent of the governed. Cuba belongs to the American system, and the question of her fate is essentially American. We cannot be indifferent to the struggle, and trust and believe that our Government stands ready to acknowledge her independence at the earliest moment that will be justified by the laws and usages of nations. Though we cannot rightfully intervene between Spain and her colony which she has so long oppressed and impoverished, our sympathies are with the Cubans, and we cannot regret any aid they may receive which does not involve a breach of the international duty of our Government. While the grand revolution in Spain is proceeding so peacefully and successfully; while the Spanish people are asserting their liberties and fortifying them by constitutional bulwarks, it is to be deeply regretted that they are denying to Cuba what they claim for themselves.

The American Revolution was also an English revolution. The struggle for liberty here reacted upon England, has gone forward there continually, and is stronger to-day than ever. One reform has succeeded another. The basis of suffrage has been widened from time to time, and has always been followed by an extension of the rights, privileges, and prosperity of the people. The institutions of England have become more liberal, just, and beneficent as the right of suffrage has been extended, and a larger number of men admitted to a voice in the government. Recently we have seen a new extension of the franchise, followed almost immediately by a movement for the disestablishment of the Irish Church. The Irish Church establishment though professedly in the interests of Protestantism, is not sustained or justified by the Protestant world, and the Protestant masses of England are demanding its repeal. The disestablishment bill has passed the House of Commons, but the lords threaten to reject it, or destroy it by modifications. It may sacrifice itself, but it cannot thereby preserve the Irish establishment. The House of Lords is tolerated only upon the condition that it will ratify the action of the Commons, and will give its formal assent to all popular movements. It possesses no real political power, and will not be permitted to obstruct the wishes of the people. Should it be rash enough to reject the disestablishment bill, it will at once inaugurate a movement for its own reörganization, and the destruction of hereditary privileges. Such a movement cannot, perhaps, be long deferred anyhow. Another reform bill will soon be demanded, making suffrage universal, or nearly so, to be followed by the disestablishment of the English Church, the abolition of the laws of primogeniture, and the final destruction of the kingly office. The mass of the English people are substantially, though not professedly, republican in sentiment. They accept the great doctrine of human rights upon which our Government is founded; and, while they yet retain the throne and the House of Lords, any attempt on the part of either to exercise positive power, or resist the popular will, would be instantly met by threats of resistance, and, if not abandoned, by revolution. The throne and the Upper House remain much like the feudal castles that yet distinguish the English landscape, emblems of departed power, curious to the view, full of historic interest, but no longer dangerous to the peace of the surrounding country. English reforms, heretofore slow, are becoming more rapid, and the English people are marching with accelerated speed to a republican government. Universal suffrage and hereditary privilege cannot exist long together. They are essentially hostile elements. The progress of suffrage in England has been resisted at every step by the aristocratic classes; but, after many years of struggle, it has arrived at that point where its further progress cannot be long delayed. Universal suffrage lies at the very summit of the hill of Difficulty, the ascent of which is rugged, slow and toilsome, but when achieved, the people will be masters of the situation. America is avenging herself upon England by gradually but surely overturning her aristocratic and hierarchic institutions by the force of her teachings and example. The principles of civil and religious liberty, crude and imperfect when first brought from England to America, having been refined, illustrated, and extended, we return them to the mother country for her adoption, laden with rich and glorious results. The spirit of American liberty is abroad in England. Her Brights, Gladstones, Forsters, and her whole host of liberal statesmen are proclaiming the doctrines of the Declaration of Independence, and verifying the saying of a celebrated Englishman, that the American Revolution guaranteed the free institutions of England. We may not live to see England a republic, but I believe our children will. The event can be predicted with as much certainty as any other in human affairs, and it is hastening on, perhaps fast enough when all things are considered.

The difficulties in the way of putting down the Rebellion were great. The rebellious States contained a population of not less than ten millions, and although nearly four millions were slaves, yet most of them, until the very conclusion of the war, constituted the laboring and producing classes, and furnished the supplies for the Rebel armies in the field, and the non-combatants at home. The territory of the rebellious States comprised an area of not less than eight hundred thousand square miles, diversified by vast ranges of mountains, deep rivers, tangled wilderness, and far-stretching swamps, and everywhere presenting natural defences, behind which a small force could hold a large one at bay. The lines of communication were necessarily of great length, and maintained with difficulty. A large portion of our forces were constantly employed in this way, and in garrisoning posts, so that it was seldom we were able to meet the enemy with superior force upon the field. These immense difficulties went far to counterbalance our superiority in population and resources, and were so great as to lead military observers throughout Europe to prophesy, almost with one accord, that we could not conquer the South. It was said there was no instance in history where so large a population, scattered over even one-third of a territory so great as that embraced by the Rebellion, had been subdued. It was said we could not conquer space; that conquest would be a geographical impossibility; that three millions of men could not garrison the South, and that when we had captured their towns and overrun the inhabited parts of their country, they would still maintain the war in morass, mountain and forest, almost impenetrable to regular armies, until the North, exhausted in blood and treasure, and broken in hope, would give up the contest. Such was the belief of leading military minds in Europe, and of the politicians of the South when the war began. These opinions seemed well-founded in reason and in history, and the suppression of the Rebellion, all things considered, may be justly regarded as the greatest of all military achievements. The fact that the Rebels fought upon their own soil, in a country with which they were familiar, protected from the approach of loyal armies by the natural advantages before described, was a full compensation for the difference between the population and resources of the two sections, and the final triumph of our arms and the suppression of the Rebellion must be sought for in other causes. What these causes were may be briefly stated:

First. In the strength, courage, and endurance imparted to armies by the conviction that they are fighting in a just and patriotic cause. The humblest privates in our army believed that they were fighting to preserve the best government in the world; to preserve liberty and extinguish slavery; in behalf of civilization and Christianity; against barbarism and inhumanity. These convictions gave inspiration, courage and hope to the army, and animated the great mass of the people of the North, who sustained the Government throughout the contest, constituting an immense moral power, in opposition to which the South had but little to offer. The people of the South had bitter prejudices, which had been carefully fostered by the designing politicians. Many of them believed in the abstract doctrine, under the Constitution, of State sovereignty and the right of secession. Some of them believed in the rightfulness of slavery, but more in its profitableness, its convenience, and its contributions to luxury and pride. But all of these constituted no moral power to inspire the patriot, nerve the soldier, give consolation in the dying hour, or determine people never to surrender, and to struggle on to the last. When, therefore, the principal armies of the Rebellion were overcome and had surrendered, the war was at an end. Hostility was not maintained in the forest and mountain as had been predicted. The convictions, hopes and purposes of the masses had been extinguished before their armies were, and although they were full of bitterness and humiliation, yet there was nothing left for which they might sacrifice their homes and the future quiet and prosperity of their lives. Their cause failed in advance of their armies and resources. The Rebel historian of the "Lost Cause," in descanting upon the subject, speaks as follows:—

"The whole fabric of Confederate defence tumbled down at a stroke of arms that did not amount to a battle. There was no last great convulsion, such as usually marks the final struggle of a people's devotion, or the expiring hours of their desperation. The word surrender travelled from Virginia to Texas. A four years' contest terminated with the smallest incident of bloodshed; it lapsed, it passed by a rapid and easy transition into a profound and abject submission. There must be some explanation of this flat conclusion of the war. It is easily found. Such a condition could only take place in the thorough demoralization of the armies and people of the Confederacy; there must have been a general decay of public spirit—a general rottenness of public affairs—when a great war was thus terminated, and a contest was abandoned so short of positive defeat, and so far from the historical necessity of subjugation."

And again he says:

"We fear that the lessons and examples of history are to the contrary, and we search in vain for one instance where a country of such extent as the Confederacy has been so thoroughly subdued by any amount of military force, unless where popular demoralization has supervened."

History records that many nations, far more exhausted than they, have struggled on to final victory. Our Revolutionary fathers, at the end of four years, defeated, exhausted and overrun, did not despair, but, animated by the justice of their cause and the belief that it would triumph because it was just, struggled on, and at the end of seven years were blessed with peace and the rich reward which shall be the inheritance of the earth. "Thrice is he armed who hath his quarrel just," and weak and defenceless are they who contend for injustice and slavery, though girt about by the mountain, the swift river and the deep wilderness.

Secondly. The armies of the North were strong in that physical endurance which is communicated by habitual labor, and by that self-reliance and confidence which free labor only can inspire. They were strong in the intelligence of the masses who filled the ranks. These men understood well the nature of the struggle in which they were engaged. They knew the vast consequences to themselves, their posterity, and to the world, depending upon the result. Their education enabled them not only to comprehend the "cause," but military operations, the condition of the Government and the country, and the decline of the spirit and strength of the enemy. In short, our armies were a vast intelligence, subject to military control, possessing clear ideas of duty, condition, consequences, and spirit and resolution commensurate to these.

We have met here to-day to dedicate this Monument to the memory of the patriotic and gallant men who fell upon this field, and to testify our love to the great cause in which they perished. Their achievements will be recorded upon the pages of history, much more enduring than stone, but we desire to present this visible evidence of our remembrance and gratitude. We are surrounded to-day by many of the surviving heroes of the battle; by many of the relatives and friends of those beloved dead, and by many thousands of our people who rejoice in the preservation, peace and prosperity of our country. That we have an united country, that we have national Government, that we have peace in all our borders, that there is liberty and protection for all, that we have bright and glorious prospects of individual happiness and national growth and power, we owe to the brave men who fell upon this and other fields. The glorious circumstance and bright auspices over and around us to-day were purchased by their blood. We are in the full enjoyment of the prize for which it was shed.

Let us increase the gratitude of our hearts by considering for a moment what would be our condition if the Rebellion had triumphed. We would have no solemn but sweet occasions like this. We would have no common country, no common name, no national flag, no glorious prospects for the future. Had the bond of union been broken, the various parts would have crumbled to pieces. We should have a slaveholding confederacy in the South; a republic on the Pacific; another in the Northwest, and another in the East. With the example of one successful secession, dismemberment of the balance would have speedily followed; and our country, once the hope of the world, the pride of our hearts, broken into hostile fragments, would have been blotted from the map, and became a byword among the nations. Let us thank Almighty God to-day that we have escaped this horrible fate. We feel as one who awakes from a terrible dream, and rejoices that he is alive. We feel as did the children of Israel, when, standing upon the shores of the Red Sea, they looked back upon the destruction from which they had been delivered.

Mr. Lincoln, standing in this place a few months after the battle, and while yet the conflict was raging, dedicated himself to his country and to the cause of liberty and union. The demon of Rebellion afterward exacted his life, but the inspiration of the words he spoke is resting upon us to-day. The great prophecy he uttered when he said, "the nation shall, under God, have a new birth of freedom," and that " the government of the people, by the people, and for the people, shall not perish from the earth," is being fulfilled. He sealed his devotion with his blood, and sacred be his memory. The eloquent Everett, who spoke here on the same occasion, and who has since passed from earth, said: "God bless the Union; it is dearer to us from the blood of brave men which has been shed in its defence." As I stood by them and listened to their inspired words, my faith was renewed in the triumph of liberty; but imagination failed to stretch forward to this auspicious day. The march of events has been faster than our thoughts, and the fruits of victory have already exceeded our most sanguine expectations.

While we pay this tribute of love and gratitude to the dead, let us not forget the surviving heroes of the battle. They, too, offered their lives, but the sacrifice was not required. The admiration, love and gratitude of the nation will attend them as they pass down the declivity of time to honored graves. In the evening of their lives they will tell the story of Gettysburg to wondering youth, who will listen as we did when our grandfathers told of Bunker Hill, Saratoga, and Yorktown. Many of them are here to-day, to review the scene of their struggle and triumph. How powerful the contrast between now and then! The dark cloud which overspread the horizon of the nation is gone, and all is brightness. The sulphurous cloud of battle, too, is gone, and there is nothing to obscure our vision of the field. The dead have returned to dust. The fields once cumbered with bodies and slippery with blood, are clothed with verdure and harvest, and to-day all is peace, beauty and repose.

We seek not to commemorate a triumph over our misguided countrymen. It is the cause we celebrate. Our triumph is theirs, and their children's children, until the latest generation. The great disturbing element has been removed. Vicious political heresies have been extirpated. The trial by wager of battle has been decided in favor of liberty and union, and all will submit. The people of the North and South have met each other face to face on many a field, have tried each other's courage, have found they are much alike in many things, have increased their mutual respect, and are now preparing to live together more fraternally than before.

The Southern States are rapidly recovering from the prostration of the war, and with their deliverance from the incubus of slavery, with free labor, with free schools, with emigration from the North and from Europe, will soon attain a prosperity and power of which they scarcely dreamed in former days. The advancing prosperity is solid, just and enduring. We rejoice in it. The bonds of Union are made indissoluble by the community of political principles, by the complete identity of domestic and commercial interests, and by a uniform system of labor, of education, and of habits of thought and action. HENCEFORTH DISUNION IS IMPOSSIBLE.

DEDICATION ODE.

FOR THE NATIONAL CEMETERY AT GETTYSBURG.

BY BAYARD TAYLOR.

I.

After the eyes that looked, the lips that spake
Here, from the shadows of impending death,
Those words of solemn breath,
What voice may fitly break
The silence, doubly hallowed, left by him?
We can but bow the head, with eyes grown dim,
And, as a nation's litany, repeat
The phrase his martyrdom hath made complete,
Noble as then but now more sadly sweet;
"Let us, the Living, rather dedicate
Ourselves to the unfinished work, which they
Thus far advanced so nobly on its way,
And save the periled State!
Let us, upon this field where they, the brave,
Their last full measure of devotion gave,
Highly resolve they have not died in vain!—
That, under God, the nation's later birth
Of Freedom, and the People's gain,
Of their own Sovereignty shall never wane
And perish from the circle of the earth!"
From such a perfect text shall Song aspire
To light its faded fire,
And into wandering music turn
Its virtue, simple, sorrowful and stern?
His voice all elegies anticipated:
For, whatsoe'er the strain,
We hear that one refrain:
"We consecrate ourselves to them, the consecrated!"

II.

After the thunder-storm our heaven is blue:
Far off, along the borders of the sky,
In silver folds the clouds of battle lie,
With soft, consoling sunlight shining through;
And round the sweeping circles of your hills
The crashing cannon thrills
Have faded from the memory of the air;
And summer pours from unexhausted fountains
Her bliss on yonder mountains:
The camps are tenantless; the breastworks bare:
Earth keeps no stain where hero-blood was poured:
The hornets, humming on their wings of lead,
Have ceased to sting, their angry swarms are dead,
And, harmless in its scabbard, rusts the sword!

III.

Oh, not till now—oh, now we dare, at last,
To give our heroes fitting consecration!
Not till the soreness of the strife is past,
And Peace hath comforted the weary Nation!
So long her sad, indignant spirit held
One keen regret, one throb of pain unquelled,
So long the land about her feet was waste,
The ashes of the burning lay upon her,
We stood beside their graves with brows abased,
Waiting the purer mood to do them honor!
They, through the flames of this dread holocaust,
The patriot's wrath, the soldier's ardor, lost;
They sit above us and above our passion,
Disparaged even by our human tears,—
Beholding truth our race, perchance, may fashion
In the slow judgment of the creeping years.
We saw the still reproof upon their faces;
We heard them whisper from the shining spaces:
" To-day ye grieve: come not to us with sorrow!
Wait for the glad, the reconciled To-morrow!
Your grief but clouds the ether where we dwell;

Your anger keeps your souls and ours apart;
But come with peace and pardon, all is well!
And come with love, we touch you, heart to heart!

IV.

Immortal Brothers, we have heard!
Our lips declare the reconciling word:
For Battle taught, that set us face to face,
The stubborn temper of the race,
And both, from fields no longer alien, come,
To grander action equally invited,—
Marshalled by Learning's tramp, by Labor's drum.
In strife that purifies and makes united!
We force to build, the powers that would destroy:
The muscles, hardened by the sabre's grasp
Now give our hands a firmer clasp:
We bring not grief to you, but solemn joy!
And, feeling you so near,
Look forward with your eyes, divinely clear,
To some sublimely-perfect, sacred year,
When sons of fathers whom ye overcame
Forget in mutual pride the partial blame,
And join with us to set the final crown
Upon your dear renown,—
The People's Union in heart and name!

V.

And yet, ye Dead!—and yet
Our clouded natures cling to one regret:
We are not all resigned
To yield, with even mind,
Our scarcely risen stars, that here untimely set.
We needs must think of history that waits
For lines that live but in their proud beginning—
Arrested promises and cheated fates—
Youth's boundless venture and its single winning.
We see the ghosts of deeds they might have done,
The phantom homes that beaconed their endeavor;

The seeds of countless lives in them begun,
That might have multiplied for us forever!
We grudge the better strain of men
That proved itself, and was extinguished then—
The field, with strength and hope so thickly sown,
Wherefrom no other harvest shall be mown ;
For all the land, within its clasping seas,
Is poorer now in bravery and beauty,
Such wealth of manly loves and energies
Was given to teach us all the free man's sacred duty.

VI.

Again 'tis they, the Dead,
By whom our hearts are comforted,
Deep as the land-blown murmurs of the waves,
The answer cometh from a thousand graves :
" Not so ! we are not orphaned of our fate !
Though life was warmest and though love were sweetest,
We still have portion in their best estate ;
Our fortune is the fairest and completest !
Our homes are everywhere ; our loves are set
In hearts of man and woman, sweet and vernal ;
Courage and Truth, the children we beget,
Unmixed of baser earth, shall be eternal.
A finer spirit in the blood shall give
The token of the lines wherein we live,—
Unselfish force, unconscious nobleness
That in the shocks of fortune stand unshaken,—
The hopes that in their very being bless,
The aspirations that to deeds awaken !
Oh, if superior virtue ye allow
To us, be sure it still is vital in you,—
That trust like ours shall ever lift the brow,
And strength like ours shall ever steel the sinew !
We are blossoms which the storm has cast
From the Spring promise of our Freedom's tree,
Pruning its overgrowths, that so, at last,
Its later fruit more bountiful shall be !—
Content, if, when the balm of Time assuages

The branch's hurt, some fragrance of our lives
In all the land survives,
And makes their memory sweet through still expanding ages!"

VII.

Thus grandly, they we mourn, themselves console us:
And, as their spirits conquer and control us,
We hear from some high realm that lies beyond,
The hero-voices of the Past respond.
From every State that reached a broader right
Through fiery gates of battle; from the shock
Of old invasions on the People's rock;
From tribes that stood, in Kings' and Priests' despite;
From graves forgotten in the Syrian sand,
Or nameless barrows of the Northern strand,
Or gorges of the Alps and Pyrenees,
Or the dark bowels of devouring seas,—
Wherever Man for Man's sake died—wherever
Death stayed the march of upward-climbing feet,
Leaving their Present incomplete,
But through far Futures crowning their endeavor.
Their ghostly voices to our ears are sent,
As when the high note of the trumpet wrings
Æolian answers from the strings
Of many a mute, unfingered instrument.
Platæan cymbals thrill for us to-day;
The horns of Sempach in our echoes play,
And nearer yet, and sharper, and more stern,
The slogan rings that startled Bannockburn;
Till from the field, made green with kindred deed,
The shields are slashed in exultation
Above the dauntless Nation,
That for a Continent has fought its Runnymede!

VIII.

Yes, for a Continent! The heart that beats
With such rich blood of sacrifice
Shall, from the Tropics, drowsed with languid heats,

To the blue ramparts of the Northern ice,
Make felt its pulses, all this young world over!—
Shall thrill and shake and sway
Each land that bourgeons in the Western day.
Whatever flag may float, whatever shield may cover,
With fuller manhood every wind is rife.
In every soil are sown the seeds of valor,
Since out of death came forth such boundless life,
Such ruddy beauty out of anguished pallor!
And that war wasted arm
Put forth to lift a sister-land from harm,
Ere the last blood upon the blade was dried,
Shall still be stretched, to shelter and to guide,
Beyond her borders, answering the need
With counsel and with deed,
Along the Eastern and the Western wave,
Still strong to smite, still beautiful to save!

IX.

Thus, in her seat secure,
Where now no distant menaces can reach her,
At last in undivided freedom pure,
She sits, the unwilling world's unconscious teacher ;
And, day by day, beneath serener skies,
The unshaken pillars of her palace rise—
The Doric shafts, that lightly upward press,
And hide in grace their giant massiveness,
What though the sword has hewn each corner-stone,
And precious blood cements the deep foundation?
Never by other force have empires grown ;
From other basis never rose a nation !
For strength is born of struggle, faith of doubt,
Of discord law, and freedom of oppression.
We hail from Pisgah, with exulting shout,
The Promised Land below us, bright with sun,
And deem its pastures won,
Ere toil and blood have earned us their possession !
Each aspiration of our human earth
Becomes an act through keenest pangs of birth ;

Each force, to bless, must cease to be a dream,
And conquer life through agony supreme;
Each inborn right must outwardly be tested
By stern material weapons, ere it stand
In the enduring fabric of the land,
Secured for those who yielded it, and those who wrested!

X.

This they have done for us who slumber here,
Awake, alive, though now so dumbly sleeping;
Spreading the board, but tasting not its cheer,
Sowing, but never reaping;—
Building, but never sitting in the shade
Of the strong mansion they have made;—
Speaking their words of life with mighty tongue,
But hearing not the echo, million-voiced
Of brothers who rejoiced,
From all our river-vales and mountains flung!
So take them, Heroes of the songful Past!
Open your ranks, let every shining troop
Its phantom banners droop,
To hail Earth's noblest martyrs, and her last!
Take them, O Fatherland!
Who, dying, conquered in thy name;
And, with a grateful hand,
Inscribe their deed who took away thy blame,—
Give, for their grandest all, thine insufficient fame!
Take them, O God! our Brave,
The glad fulfillers of Thy dread decree;
Who grasped the sword for Peace, and smote to save,
And, dying here for Freedom, died for Thee!

The Benediction was pronounced by the Rev. S. S. Schmucker, D. D.

www.ingramcontent.com/pod-product-compliance
Lightning Source LLC
Chambersburg PA
CBHW030903170426
43193CB00009BA/727